A "How-To-Do-It" Book

BIRDS
TOMORROW

The Management And Enjoyment Of
The Birds of North America

by Norval R. Barger

Library of Congress Cataloging-in-Publication Data

Barger, Norval R.
   Birds tomorrow.

   (A "How-to-do-it" book)
   Bibliography: p.
   1. Birds, Protection of—North America. 2. Birds—
North America. 3. Birds, Attracting of—North America.
I. Title. II. Series.
QL681.B3117   1991   639.9'78   89-3442
ISBN 0-87961-192-8
ISBN 0-87961-193-6 (pbk.)

Books for a better world

Naturegraph Publishers, Inc.
3543 Indian Creek Road
Happy Camp, CA 96039
U.S.A.

Memories

I shall never forget the conversation I had with a professor of ornithology many years ago while I was attending high school in Virginia. Bluebirds, nesting in a box which I had put up for them in my back yard, had reared one brood and were now in the process of feeding their second brood. Unfortunately, the male bluebird, which regularly assisted with the care of the nestlings, was killed. To my surprise, on the following day, some members of the first brood which had remained in the vicinity began to feed the young of the second brood. My question of the professor was, "Do young bluebirds always assist their parents in this way, or did these particular birds feel sorry for their widowed mother?" He explained that young bluebirds are likely to help out in this way at any time and suggested that I record my observations while they were fresh in mind. "But," I protested, "if it is already known that bluebirds behave in this way, would my notes have any value?" "You never know when they will be useful," he replied. Well, I have never regretted keeping a notebook. Many of the things which I shall write about in this book are taken from my notebook. I hope they will be useful to you, my readers, and a source of encouragement toward further investigation.

Foreword

This book is *for the birds,* but I hope the *people* will get their chance at it first. Throughout most of my life it has been my good fortune to work in the field of wildlife management. When on the job much emphasis was placed upon the management of our birds, but the more I worked at this, the more I realized that I was not managing birds—I was managing *people.* Hence, this book.

In order to help preserve our birdlife for future generations, my hope is to stimulate the thinking of my readers so they will take intelligent action. I am encouraged by the fact many people are interested in wildlife today. A recent survey indicates that more than fifty million wildlife observers reside in the United States alone. In any event, I have never met a wildlife observer who was not interested in birds.

When preparing an outline for this book, I decided from the outset to take a middle course. The professional worker does not need my help, and readers on the elementary level are rapidly disappearing from the scene now that the science of ornithology has come of age. No effort has been made to exhaust the subject (this would take several books) but I have included those things which I believe will be most helpful to the average participant.

Regarding the names of birds, I am following the American Ornithologists' Union Check-list of North American Birds (sixth edition, 1983). There are a number of changes from previous lists, but if the new name is unrecognizable, I have included in parentheses the former name. It is still the practice to capitalize the names of birds in order to set them apart.

My photographs are selected to illustrate the text. Thus the birds shown may not be arranged according to size; but I have compensated for this by giving their measurements in centimeters and inches, near their photographs.

Customarily bird behavior is described in the same way that we describe human behavior. This is for convenience sake only, as we do not mean to convey the idea that birds necessarily behave like people. (Only recently, an elderly gentleman quipped that the only similarity he had noticed was that the females appear to ignore the males!)

I am indebted to my fellow wildlife workers for keeping me up-to-date while on the job and while preparing this book. Also, I am grateful to the members of my family for helping me in every way; particularly with my photography. Lastly I wish to give special thanks to Laurence Jahn, Chandler Robbins, Karen Rusch, and David Willard, who were kind enough to look at parts of my manuscript or color slides in advance and to make suggestions of various kinds. Any errors remaining, however, are my own.

Table of Contents

Chapter 1

FUN THINGS TO DO

"Everywhere we turn, we find some new interest in birds, some new pleasure in watching them."
—Milton P. Skinner

Back Yard Activities

A recent survey conducted among those who feed birds indicates that about two hundred million dollars are spent annually for bird feed in North America. In most shopping centers today are displays of bird feed, bird feeders, bird baths, and bird houses; and many nurseries take pride in furnishing trees and shrubs that attract birds. There can be no doubt that more interest is shown in back yard birding today than ever before.

Feeders For The Back Yard

Feeders may be selected on the basis of a bird's habits. A chickadee, for example, will come to the feeder, pick up a sunflower seed, and carry it to a convenient perch where it can open it easily. Thus a feeder of almost any style will do for it. Purple Finches, on the other hand, usually sit in the feeder while eating, so more space is required, either in the size of the feeder or in the number of feeders provided. Moreover, Purple Finches usually come in flocks. Jays, as a rule, dominate the feeders and drive the more timid birds away. To avoid this problem, feeders of more than one style and location may be tried. The Brown Creeper, in common with woodpeckers, obtains its food from the upright surface of tree trunks, so racks containing suet may be bound closely to trees for its benefit. Doves, quail, and many of our native sparrows habitually feed on the ground. This, of course, brings up the question of ground predators. A partial solution can be found by mounting a broad, *flat* board on a post that is tall enough to keep them down. It is not the complete answer, because many ground-loving birds hesitate to fly even to such an elevation.

Feeders may also be selected on the basis of convenience. During inclement weather, it is often desirable to replenish the food supply without going outdoors. One solution to this problem is to use window sill feeders. These are obtainable either with or without glass roofs, and the latter can be hinged if desired. If a person happens to live on the second floor, and it appears that the birds are reluctant to come so high, a "trolley car" arrangement can be implemented. The car runs below a wire, pulley style, from a tree to a window so that it can be drawn a little closer each day, thereby bringing the birds to the window. Food supplies are replenished from the window.

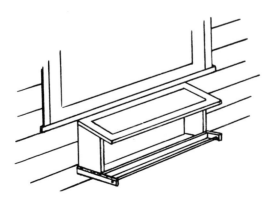

Window Sill Feeder. The birds may be observed through the glass roof.

Kinds of Food

What to feed will vary with the seasons as well as with the kinds of birds to be expected in a given locality. Because they are easily obtained, seeds play a dominant part in all feeding programs. Included on the list are sunflower, corn, wheat, oats, millet, rice, milo, buck-wheat, hemp, soybean, grass, pumpkin, squash, and Niger seeds. In addition, weed seeds (screenings), sometimes available from feed mills, may be used. Incidentally, I prefer to buy bird food under the label of *feed*, rather than *seed*, as the latter may be treated with a dangerous substance. Grit or sand is desirable as an aid to digestion and for its mineral content. In order to have it available during periods of ice and snow when it is most needed, a supply should be stored ahead of time.

Beef suet, perhaps should be mentioned next. It is important especially to those species that do not regularly eat grain. As a further help to the soft-billed species, fruits such as raisins, currants, berries, cut apples, cut oranges, and bits of banana may be offered. Nuts form an important part of the diet of many species of birds. Almost any kind obtainable may be used, but acorns, for example, should be cracked so that the smaller birds can eat the meats. Peanuts serve well, either in or out of the shell, but they should not be salted. I, personally, would not recommend peanut butter, as birds are inclined to choke on it.

Most of the food should be served raw as this is the most natural way. I would not rule out bread entirely but this item can be overused. Neither would I rule out the use of table scraps entirely, although they, like bread, may contain salt. A few species of birds relish salt and seem to need it, but the majority appear to get along better without it.

Food For Hummingbirds

While hummingbirds can be easily attracted to the flower border or porch vine where natural blossoms abound, they respond quite well to artificial feeders. Such devices are available on the market. Usually they are made of red or orange material as the birds seem attracted to these colors. Whether all species respond in the same way to bright colors is debatable, for dull colors have been used with success in some regions. Such devices can be handmade—from medicine containers or vials, for example—but there is danger involved. The birds may reach in so far that they cannot get out. Thus no device having a large mouth should be more than five centimeters (2 in.) in depth. Hummingbirds are inclined to be beligerent around their feeders so it may be desirable to set up several of them, widely spaced.

Not all hummingbird fanciers use the same formula for the food, but one part sugar to four parts water is perfectly acceptable. Color is not needed if the feeder has color. I do not recommend using synthetic sweeteners.

While in southern California, I became acquainted with a method of preventing bees from swarming into the artificial containers in use at the Tucker Bird Sanctuary. Mr. Tucker, who created the sanctuary, had made metal caps for the containers, and through each of the caps several holes were bored. This arangement permitted the hummingbirds to feed, while the bees were kept out. Of course, it was necessary to fill the containers regularly, for the birds were able to reach down only for a distance of little over one centimeter (½ inch).

Certain other birds have a hankering for the hummingbird's formula. While in southern Arizona, I noticed that Scott's Oriole and the Western Tanager were fond of it. In this instance, the formula was colored red with food coloring.

Keep all hummingbird feeders out of the reach of squirrels.

Problem Areas In Feeding Programs

Many years ago, a man came to me to borrow a trap. He complained that he had a squirrel problem. "How many squirrels do you have?" I asked. "About six or seven," he replied. "Help yourself to the trap," I insisted. About three weeks later he returned with the trap, and a look of discouragement on his face. "How many squirrels did you trap?" "Forty-three," was his reply. "How many do you have left in the yard?" "Six or seven," he sighed. (He lived in the city where there were many squirrels awaiting their opportunity to move into a vacant territory.)

It is useless to try to eliminate squirrels on an urban property. I feed them in one end of my yard where the birds are not likely to gather in numbers. It is necessary to keep them off my bird feeders, though. I have a cone-shaped piece of metal (reversed) on the poles, and it is placed high enough so that the squirrels cannot jump above it when the snow is deep. Another method that works quite well is to hang the feeders on a wire, strung like a clothes line. It must be a long wire, though, or the squirrels will find a way to get to the feeders.

What to do about the cat problem is a perennial question among bird lovers. At one time, a neighbor of mine owned a cat which was well fed at home, the same being demonstrated by the appearance of the animal throughout the year. Nevertheless, during bird migrations, this cat would line up several dead birds on the garage floor every night. Thus it is useless to try to change the habits of the cat. Many cities now have ordinances requiring that pet cats must be on leash if they are out of the house, and this is of some help. In most neighborhoods, though, it is still necessary to guard the feeders and other bird facilities in the same way as for squirrels.

What about predatory birds? Feeding programs usually serve to concentrate birds, with the result that hawks, owls, shrikes, and other meat-eaters may make themselves a nuisance. Inasmuch as most predatory birds are given legal protection today, a person cannot kill them. There is a solution, however, as licensed bird banders can be called upon to trap the offending birds and release them at distant points.

Another problem that can beset the person who feeds birds on a large scale is *disease.* Large concentrations of birds in the same place, day after day, set the stage for outbreaks of disease. (Salmonellosis is a well-known example.) Small concentrations can get into difficulty too, if the feeders and surroundings are allowed to gather filth and mold. The disease problem creeps up slowly and may never be recognized, as sickly birds often crawl into a crevice or other out-of-the-way places to die. Moreover, if it is recognized, the solution may be hard to find. The best course to follow is to maintain a *clean* operation of *moderate* size.

When to begin feeding sometimes becomes a problem. I usually delay my winter feeding program until after the majority of the migrants have left and the winter residents have established their feeding patterns. In this way I do not entice migrants to risk a winter that is too severe for them, and I do not get more than my share of winter residents. Of course, this system need not apply in all localities. In fact, a year-round feeding program may be in order—it depends upon the local conditions.

In the northern parts of our country, any winter feeding program that is begun should be continued throughout the late winter and early spring as this is the most critical season for birds. Natural food is scarce and the birds may have become dependent upon our help. Also, during long vacations on the part of the operator, provision should be made for a continuous supply of food. When blizzards come, I always try to clear away the snow promptly from my feeders as this certainly is a critical time.

Nuisance boarders sometimes become a problem around feeders. I have found that European Starlings will carry away large chunks of suet if it is not well tied down. Holes in a screen or rack that are two centimeters (¾ inch) square will satisfy most of our native birds and at the same time protect the suet from such inroads. Suet is attractive to many kinds of birds, including such species as the Northern Cardinal and Northern Mockingbird, so not all suet racks should be set up for Brown Creepers and woodpeckers. I have hung suet racks on poles and from clothes lines. In Wisconsin where I have spent most of my life, I make my suet racks of wood. If they are made of metal, they stick to my skin when the temperature drops to thirty degrees below zero Celsius (—20 F.), and I fear that such metal may stick to the bird's eyes. Suet tied next to the bark of a tree may, in time, cause the bark to rot. Hence it is well to change its location periodically. Beef suet is commonly used, but other kinds may be relished.

Some people are plagued with House Sparrows about their feeders. Recently, while watching a Fox Sparrow scratch among the empty hulls of sunflower seeds, I saw a House Sparrow jump in and seize a seed which the Fox Sparrow had located after considerable effort. As House Sparrows are unprotected and generally considered to be pests, their numbers can be controlled by any legal means. They should not be poisoned though, as beneficial creatures will also be destroyed. Small bird feeders that twirl around are said to deter House Sparrows and European Starlings. I have never experimented with them.

All birds hesitate to enter areas where they sense that they will be cornered. Hence it is best to have openings on more than one side when designing a feeder. If a lean-to style feeder is constructed on the ground, there should be openings on two ends so that the birds can escape from their potential ground enemies. Some *escape cover* such as shrubs, trees, or vines are essential to any feeding program. Birds need refuge from their enemies, and such cover may also help to prevent death by exposure to the elements. In this connection, feeders serve best if they can be protected from the prevailing winds.

Why Feed The Birds?

This may sound like a superfluous question at first glance, and yet it is asked daily. Perhaps the main reason why people feed birds is because they enjoy having them nearby. We cannot say that the birds need it, for they got along quite well before the country was settled. It can be a hinderance if it is done in a careless manner. Some people like to have the bird's help in controlling insects about the premises. Others are interested in conducting research. Certainly it is a good introduction to what may later lead to a career in ornithology. Why do Northern Cardinals feed early and late in the day? I have found them at my feeder when it was too dark for most birds to be abroad. Why does the Common Grackle wet the bread before eating it? I have seen this bird take bread to the bird bath as a regular routine. These are examples of questions that whet the imagination.

Getting Started

In some localities it is difficult to get birds interested in feeders. This may be because of the abundance of natural foods in the neighborhood (this was my problem in the South), or it may be that there is too much competition from nearby feeders. Success will come, though, if one has the patience to continue. It may be desirable to use open-type feeders at first, as they attract birds more readily than those with roofs. In those regions where snow is likely to cover the food, roofs made of glass or other transparent materials may be helpful.

Water Supplies

While in Rockport, Texas, some time ago, a well-known ornithologist demonstrated to me how helpful the sound of dripping water could be in attracting birds. It was a simple device. A pail of water was hung on the lower branch of a tree above a bird bath; in the bottom of this pail was a small hole through which a screw had been loosely inserted. By adjusting this screw, water drops of the desired size could be produced. I have tried this system at my own place with good results.

On display everywhere are bird baths of the pedestal type. Most are reasonably priced and well adapted to the needs of the smaller birds. I have found it best to purchase one that is joined together in one heavy piece, for if the parts are separate, a squirrel will knock down the bowl. As song birds differ greatly in size, it is helpful to set up a deep bowl, thirteen or fifteen centimeters (5 or 6 inches) deep at the center, for the larger species, and a shallow bowl, eight or ten centimeters (3 or 4 inches), for the smaller species. The water should be kept clean and fresh. If it freezes, heating devices can be purchased.

Very elaborate bird baths or fountains can also be constructed. In order to produce a continuous waterfall, for example, one can use an aquarium pump. If one is so fortunate as to have a stream running through his property, many beautiful arrangements can be made.

Occasionally we hear of owls drowning in rain barrels, but I suspect such accidents are rare, for birds in general seem to be very cautious about entering water. Robins, for instance, will first gingerly stick their bills into the water as though to test it. In this connection, I have found that birds hesitate to bathe in a device made of slippery material such as new metal, for they cannot gain a solid foothold on it.

Birds have difficulty flying when they are wet, so they are vulnerable to their enemies at this time. The best solution to this problem is to place the water devices near trees and shrubs to which the birds can flee. The water will be seen more readily by the birds, however, if the immediate area above the bird bath is kept open.

As some species are inclined to fight over the use of the water, I have my devices well scattered in the yard. In this way many birds can be accommodated at the same time. While on the subject of baths, I might add that many species of birds enjoy *dust bathes.* Thus a few bare spots of loose soil can be maintained for this purpose.

Bird Houses and Similar Devices

When I was in the fifth grade I wrote a composition on how the bluebirds had discovered my bird house. It was the only piece of writing I can remember on which I received any commendation. I was so impressed by the ethereal beauty of these birds that I could not keep it to myself.

Eastern Bluebird, *Sialia sialis.* (male) The male does not assist with the chores of nest building and incubation, but he does feed the female while she is incubating. He also feeds and cares for the young. As the bluebird often raises two broods per season, the female is free to start the second nest while the male watches over the first brood. 18cm. (7")

Great Crested Flycatcher, *Myiarchus crinitus.* In many parts of its range, this flycatcher will dwell in areas of scattered trees. Sometimes it finds woodpecker cavities here, but often it is dependent upon bird houses, preferably those that are made of natural wood (or bark covered). It has a strong homing instinct, so once it has found a bird house, it is likely to return. 22cm. (8.5")

Purple Finch, *Carpodacus purpureus.* (male) Purple Finches are popular with those people who feed the birds in winter. They come in large flocks and often sing (twitter) merrily in the trees after they have had a good dinner. As spring approaches, the males sing a louder and more musical song which bears some resemblance to that of the Warbling Vireo. 15 cm. (6")

Grain Feeder. It is possible to purchase feeders of this style, but they are not difficult to construct. The grain flows out at the lower edge of the glass so that the birds can reach it when they perch on the platform. One side of the roof is hinged so that it can be raised when grain is replaced.

I believe that in anyone's bird house program, the bluebird ranks first. I shall have more to say on this subject under "Bluebird House Trails." As far as the back yard is concerned, certain conditions must be met. At my place in Virginia, I had spacious lawns and neighboring property that was largely open. This was ideal for bluebirds. Unfortunately, this is not the case in many neighborhoods. Cities, especially, are usually too crowded. Urbanites must, therefore, settle for such birds as House Wrens, among the cavity nesters. If there is a chance for bluebirds, however, it is best to omit the wren houses, for wrens do not get along well with bluebirds. Bird house specifications are listed by species in Appendix A. The material that immediately follows is more general in nature.

How To Build Bird Houses

It is possible to purchase bird houses on the market, but, differing from feeders and bird baths, they may not be equipped with all of the desired features. It is often necessary for a person to construct his own.

All houses need to be checked periodically for House Sparrows and other nuisances, and all should be cleaned out at least once a year, so a roof board may be hinged or left removable for this purpose. Because of the House Sparrow nuisance, perches should be left off the houses, except in the case of the Purple Martin. It is nice to paint martin houses for appearance sake, and the birds do not object, but the other houses can be left unpainted. In fact, many species seem to prefer a natural-looking house—one of either weathered wood or bark-covered slabs. All enclosed houses should be built with a single compartment, except in the case of the Purple Martin and certain other swallows.

Woodpeckers, owls, and other birds that build no

Bluebird House

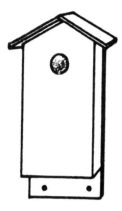

Wren House

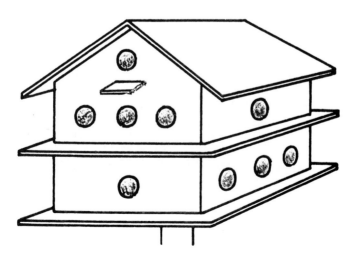

Martin House

House Wren, *Troglodytes aedon.* Of all our wrens, the House Wren is the best known. It has a wide range and will settle down wherever it can find a suitable cavity for its nest. Many people put up houses for it nowadays as they enjoy hearing it sing. This may occur in the suburbs of cities as well as elsewhere. 13 cm. (5″)

Robin Shelf. Robins are easily attracted to shelves and often such species as phoebes will use them. If they are to be placed under the eaves of a building, the roof will not be needed. The floor is 18 x 18 cm. (7 x 7 in.); the roof 20 cm. (8 in.) above the floor; and the shelf may be mounted 2 to 6 m. (7 to 20 ft.) above the ground. Mud is needed.

Brown Creeper, *Certhia americana.* Although the Brown Creeper is found occasionally in company with others of its kind, and often with birds of similar feeding habits, it is essentially a *loner.* Being equipped with stiff tail-feathers, it climbs up the tree trunks somewhat in woodpecker-fashion, looking for insects, their larvae, and eggs. When it reaches the top of a given tree in its search for food, it often drops abruptly to the base of another tree to begin anew. 14 cm. (5.5″)

Brown Creeper House. Unlike many species, Brown Creepers normally nest behind loose bark— not in cavities such as woodpeckers drill. The house shown here permits the birds to enter from two sides as they seem to prefer such an arrangement. Inside floor dimensions are 6 x 8 cm. (2½ x 3¼ in.). Attach rather high in tree so that mammals cannot easily jump to it.

23

nests, require something to hold their eggs together. It is suggested, therefore, that a generous supply of sawdust or wood shavings be inserted before the houses are put up. A mirror placed on the inside wall, opposite the entrance opening of the house, is said to be a deterrant to European Starlings. I have not experimented with this; the mirror may discourage desirable species as well.

To use clear plastic or glass for the roof is a scheme that may have some value against House Sparrows as they are less tolerant of light from above than are many of our native species. Some experimenters have provided sky lights in the roof by means of openings covered with wire netting, but this allows the rain to fall in.

Getting Them Into Place

How many to put up and for which species are questions that have to be answered on the basis of local conditions. We will discuss a few general problems, however. Houses should never be mounted on poles which have been coated with creosote (such as utility poles), as this substance inhibits the hatching of eggs. Woodpeckers, in particular, are likely to transfer this material from the pole to their eggs. Houses may tilt forward, but never backward, for, in the latter case, the young of certain species may not be able to get out. When a heavy martin house is put up, it is a good idea to hinge the pole near ground level so that the house can be easily let down for annual cleaning.

It is not a simple matter to keep mammallian predators from climbing to the houses. One of the most effective means is the inverted metal cone which is often used. It is not feasible everywhere, however, so researchers have thought of other plans, some of which are quite effective, if not the entire solution.

I like to locate the entrance door near the top of the box, as far above the floor as the species will tolerate (the box itself is tall), so that animals such as the raccoon cannot reach down to the nest and its contents, even though they extend their entire "arm" into the entrance. This helps with those species such as the bluebird, which build their nests at floor level; it does not help with those species such as the House Wren, which bolster the nest itself to the level of the entrance door. Some operators double or even triple the thickness of the wood through which the entrance door is cut in an effort to shorten the reach of the animal's "arm." This may have application with those species which bolster their nests to the level of the entrance door. Locating the entrance door near the top of the box (for those species that build their nest in the bottom) has a further advantage in that it forces the young to remain in the nest a day or two longer than otherwise, thereby aiding their survival. In my experience the cowbird is less likely to enter a deep box than one that is shallow.

The wall of a building is a comparatively safe place for bird houses as mammals do not normally find it easy to climb them. (This is assuming that the roof of the building is too high up for the animals to drop down from it to the bird house.) Another method which has been tried with a measure of success is to attach the house to a tight wire which has been stretched between two trees or posts. European Starlings seem to have a preference for shade when nesting, so houses placed in the sun may be ignored by them. As one means of discouraging House Sparrows, some people mount their bluebird houses at heights of about one meter (3 ft.) above the ground. I do not favor such low heights as almost any mammal can become a nuisance under such circumstances.

White-breasted Nuthatch,
Sitta carolinensis. (female)
Recently, a pair of these nuthatches set up house-keeping in a bird house that I had put up for wrens. First, the entrance had to be enlarged; the female did this. Next, she had to remove daily, dry grass which a House Sparrow insisted upon bringing in. Once, she could not get a large piece of nesting material into the entrance, so she placed it on the roof. The male did a lot of bill-sweeping near the nest as though this would help. (In fairness to the male, though, he did bring food regularly.) 14 cm. (5.5″)

Common Redpoll. "What do you know about it?" "Just because you are decked out in pink, you think you know everything."

Red-headed Woodpecker, *Melanerpes erythrocephalus.* As soon as this woodpecker constructs its nest cavity in a dead tree (usually located in an open area) its troubles begin. The European Starling moves in, or attempts to do so. Of course, the woodpecker can eat the eggs of the starling, but there is the grass nest of the interloper to contend with. 23 cm. (9″)

Pine Siskin, *Carduelis pinus.* For the winter, Pine Siskins partly vacate the colder parts of their range, some of the birds drifting well down into the United States and Mexico. October seems to be the peak month for this southward migration. At this time, they can be attracted to the winter bird feeders by means of sunflower seeds and smaller seeds. 13 cm. (5″)

27

When To Put Them Up

Bird houses should be put up about thirty days before eggs are normally expected. This varies geographically. In the case of migratory species, the houses may be put up on the date the desired species arrives. Of course, bird houses can be put up at any time, and most can stay in place once they are mounted, but to avoid occupancy by unwanted species it is advantageous to put them up as late in the season as possible.

I have found that subzero weather is a poor time to attach bird houses to trees. To bore a hole or to drive a nail into frozen wood is difficult; attaching them with wire is often more feasible.

Care And Maintenance Of The Houses

In my back yard is a bird house which I built for chickadees. These birds often visited it, but I noticed that they never attempted to get in. Finally, I decided to investigate, and to my surprise, I found that a flying squirrel had taken up residence there. Its nest was constructed of fine strips of bark. As this mammal is nocturnal in habits, I had never seen it in the vicinity.

On my bluebird trail, I have always found white-footed mice occupying my houses at about the time the bluebirds return from the South. Often it has been the mother mouse and her full compliment of young.

I have in my exhibit a coconut shell in which a House Wren nested. Late in the summer of the year in which it was occupied, I noticed that all activity on the part of the birds had subsided. I did not look into the cavity until the next season, but I found, spread out over the eggs, the skeleton of the mother wren. Above her was a nest of the paper wasp. Apparently, the mother had borne the stings of the wasps rather than neglect her eggs.

I take it for granted, therefore, that all bird lovers will clean their bird houses shortly before the birds are ready to build their nests. Other chores that may be looked after at the same time are to replenish the supply of sawdust in the houses that need it, to attach all houses securely once again to their supports, and to move to better locations those houses which are not being occupied by the desired species. During the course of the nesting season, too, there may be need for moving some of the bird houses. It has been found, for example, that certain snakes, after robbing a bird's nest, will return at a later date. Any bird that might rear a late-season brood there would be subject to a repeat performance.

Why Put Up Bird Houses?

The underlying reason, of course, is to help those species that are in trouble. There are a number of ramifications to this. It would be nice, for example, if we could increase the populations of our woodpeckers, not only for the benefit of the woodpeckers themselves but in order to take advantage of the chain reaction that would follow. More woodpeckers would dig more cavities, which, in turn, could be used by more of those species that cannot excavate their own. Most, if not all available cavities, are currently occupied by European Starlings or House Sparrows, which are not wanted. The starlings not only use old cavities made by the wood-peckers, they also usurp new cavities in which the owners are about to lay their eggs. In those regions where dead trees are scarce, woodpeckers often resort to utility poles for nesting purposes and to the siding of dwellings for winter quarters. This of course, is damaging to property. The hope is to alleviate such damage by putting up more bird houses. Important research is often conducted through the medium of bird houses.

Hairy Woodpecker,
Picoides villosus. (male) The Hairy Woodpecker is more retiring in its habits than the Downy Woodpecker, often resorting to the more primitive forests, whether they be in the uplands or in the swamps. Once it has established its territory here, it is likely to stay with it year after year. 24cm. (9.5″)

American Redstart, *Setophaga ruticilla.* (male) The American Redstart, the bird with the flashing wings and tail, is one of our best-known warblers. It is called *redstart* because of its similarity to the European bird by the same name. Its songs vary in pattern, but all have a *weechy* sound. (First-year males do not show the brilliant colors of the adults.) 13cm. (5″)

White-throated Sparrow, *Zonotrichia albicollis.* White-throated Sparrows come in two color phases, regardless of sex. In the adult, the head may be striped with black and white, or with brown and buff, but the *white* of the throat is usually discernable in either case. Also a small, yellow spot is usually present in front of the eye. (I took my picture in May.) 18 cm. (7″)

Bay-breasted Warbler, *Dendroica castanea.* (male) The light-buffy patch on the side of the neck distinguishes this species. Its song is surprisingly weak in character for the size of the bird, so it may not be noticed. It bears some resemblance to those of the Cape May and Blackburnian warblers. We know the species as a late migrant. Its winter range lies in Central America and northern South America. 14 cm. (5.5″) **31**

A Question

What does one do about desirable species which are incompatible? I have already pointed out how the House Wren will disrupt the nesting of bluebirds. When I was living in Virginia, I was elated when a pair of Great Crested Flycatchers started a nest in one of my bird houses. They were not able to continue, though, because a male Eastern Bluebird which had staked out a claim in my yard harassed them continually. Perhaps I should have spaced my houses farther apart.

Whenever bird houses are mentioned, we often think of song birds. Although they are important, they do not complete the picture. I have also included in Appendix A plans for houses for the larger species. I am sure that those people who own large tracts of land, or have access to them, will want to cater also to the larger birds.

Devices For Open Nesters

Those birds that nest in shrubs and trees normally find crotches or other niches in which to build, but the back yard birder can make his plantings more attractive for this purpose by careful pruning. In Europe, many ornithologists have gone a step further by making up "witches brooms" which can be attached within the shrubs or trees. These are essentially forks constructed of wire to imitate a natural crotch, but more inviting and safe. Here, as in the placement of bird houses, caution is in order, for we usurp the bird's prerogative of site selection. If we are poor judges of site, and a predator comes along to destroy the birds, we find ourselves in an embarrassing position.

Planting For The Birds

Many years ago, while living in Virginia, I watched the birds at a red mulberry tree for a period of two hours on a summer afternoon. During this time, twelve species came to feed on its fruit. Truly, I thought, this was a valuable tree. I did not know until recently that redpolls would eat the seeds of the mock-orange, but a Common Redpoll came regularly one winter to such a shrub by my window. In late winter, Pine Grosbeaks occasionally feed on the crab apples in my front yard, but I notice that when danger threatens, they take refuge in a nearby Norway spruce. Many examples of plants useful to the birds can be cited.

When planting for birds, food-bearing plants usually are thought of, and rightly so, but it is not necessary to plant these to the total exclusion of the other kind, for all furnish cover, and all harbor insects which serve as food. Both deciduous and coniferous (or other ever-green) types, whether food-bearing or otherwise, are useful, the latter (evergreen) being especially so in winter.

Details on food plants and the birds they attract are furnished in Appendix B; the following material is more general in nature. We are concerned with such things as trees, shrubs, vines, and ground cover (including flowers). Among these are plants that furnish berries, seeds, buds, blossoms, leaves, and nectar.

Plant Arrangements

During some years, White-crowned Sparrows visit my back yard where they find food on the open lawn. I notice that when danger threatens they scurry immediately for cover in the shrubbery that grows along the edges. Thus it seems that at least two kinds of habitat are useful to this species.

Pine Grosbeak, *Pinicola enucleator.* (male) This species acquired its name many years ago (it lives also in the Old World), but the small size of its beak reminds us that the bird feeds on tree buds, small fruits, and insects, as well as on seeds. The bird shown here appears to be a first-year male. (I photographed it late in February.) 23 cm. (9″)

Common Redpoll, *Carduelis flammea.* (male) This northern visitor can be attracted to the feeding tray. I have found that it will eat sunflower seeds and the smaller grains that are commonly sold on the market. Also it will utilize foods produced on ornamental plantings such as birch, mock-orange, and aster. In the wild, it relishes the seeds of evening primrose, so this plant could be added to the flower border. 14 cm. (5.5″)

Wilson's Warbler, *Wilsonia pusilla.* (male) In migration, this warbler is seen often in the lower branches of trees or in shrubbery, but during the nesting period, it is likely to be found in thickets of alder or willow. The black cap sets the male apart, but the female has only an indication of the dark cap. Elliot Coues named the species for Alexander Wilson. 13 cm. (5")

Ruby-crowned Kinglet, *Regulus calendula.* (male) Kinglets (little kings) are so-named because of the colorful crowns of the males. In the subject species, this crown patch is not always visible and the female does not have such an adornment, but the birds can be recognized by their ways. They twitch their wings nervously, and this is often accompanied by a gritty, wrenlike call. 10 cm. (4")

A landowner may arrange the habitat to appeal either to certain species or to birds in general, but, in either case, it seems that the key word is *variety*. As variety can be attained whether the landscape plan is formal or informal, either plan will suit the bird's needs. Professional landscape plans, as we commonly see them today, serve very well.

Clumps of trees or shrubs, or mixtures of both are of more value to the birds than single plants or single rows of plants, as they offer better protection. Three coniferous trees, for example, grouped closely as a unit, offer great security. Deciduous shrubs or trees, especially those with thorns, also serve well when grouped in clusters. For variety, deciduous and coniferous and other evergreen plants can be grouped as one unit.

It is well known that certain plants, particularly those that bear food, do well in sunlight. Thus "island" arrangements are best, but the outer edges of large plantations also serve well.

When snow is deep, bare ground often can be found under coniferous and other evergreen trees or shrubs, and this is a boon to juncos and the other birds that commonly feed from the ground. Vines and vine tangles are valuable. Many varieties offer both food and cover. Even when they lack fruit, as sometimes occurs in shady locations, they are still useful. I think of the fox-grape in this connection.

In winter, food-bearing plants often have their fruits blown off by strong winds. In the upper Midwest, various crab apples suffer in this way, and they are among the most valuable plants from the standpoint of the birds in late winter and early spring. If possible, such plants should be located in the more protected spots.

Garden flowers serve many purposes. We often think of hummingbirds as their patrons, but other species also find them useful. I have noticed, for example, that goldfinches are fond of zinnia seeds.

In order to avoid disappointment at a later date, consider in advance the speed of growth and the maximum size which the various trees and shrubs will attain.

Selecting The Plants

The variety and quantity of plants to be selected will be influenced by the amount of space available and the bird species to be catered to. In general it is best to select only those varieties which have been tried and tested locally. These can be either native or exotic. If advice is needed, it usually can be obtained from the personnel of a nursery, arboretum, or governmental agency. Local soil conditions, whether a given plant is considered to be a pest or disease carrier locally, and whether more than one specimen must be planted to obtain fruit, are some of the questions that should be considered.

Maintenance

Maintenance of a bird sanctuary does not differ greatly from that of the average home property. Actually, it may be more simple than one would expect. It is not desirable, for example, to rake the leaves on all parts of the property, as mulch is very useful to birds. Neither is it desirable to mow all of the grass, for some birds may wish to nest in it.

Occasional pruning of shrubs or trees may be called for to help the birds and periodic changes may have to be made when plants outgrow their usefulness. If the local laws permit, it is helpful to leave in place a few dead trees or dead branches of trees, not only for nesting purposes, but also for the insects they will

Nashville Warbler, *Vermivora ruficapilla.* (male) This warbler is easily identified as it has a white eye ring, *grayish* head, and yellow throat. The song of the male, often heard, is a help too, as it is composed of two parts, the second of which is the lowest in pitch. There is no significance in the name, except that the first specimen was discovered near Nashville, Tennessee, by Wilson. 13 cm. (5″)

Orange-crowned Warbler, *Vermivora celata.* This species is one of the most widespread warblers in North America, but it is not very well-known. The reason for this, no doubt, is its nondescript appearance. (Its orange-brown crown patch does not often show in the field.) Moreover, the various geographical forms vary slightly in color. The song resembles that of the Chipping Sparrow, but it is weak in volume. (Photograph was taken in Wisconsin.) 13 cm. (5″)

Gray Catbird, *Dumetella carolinensis.* The nest of the Gray Catbird is generally built in a shrub or small tree, somewhat removed from the disturbances of civilization. Mated pairs, it is interesting to note, may return to the same home site in successive years. The song bears some resemblance to those of our thrashers, but the phrases are seldom repeated. 23 cm. (9″)

Solitary Vireo, *Vireo solitarius.* Several geographical forms are now combined under the present name of this vireo. Names such as Blue-headed, Mountain, and Plumbeous, among others, linger in our minds. Perhaps *Solitary* is appropriate for the species, though, as the birds do appear to shun the habitations of man, and instead, to cling to the solitude of the forests; often coniferous. (Photograph was taken in Wisconsin.) 14 cm. (5.5″)

harbor for the birds. To remove quickly a tree or shrub because it fails to blossom may be a mistake as the plant may be too young, suffering from a late frost, or simply having an *off* year. In some localities or situations it may be possible to leave a portion of the property undisturbed. The borders of streams lend themselves to this kind of treatment.

Getting Started

If a person owns property that is virtually devoid of vegetations, he can begin to attract birds by building *temporary cover.* Cast off Christmas trees can be stuck upright into the ground, and unwanted brush can be arranged in piles to resemble shrubs. I allow fox-grape vines to grow over my brush piles as they cover them quickly. One's success with birds in a temporary plan of this kind may be affected by the general condition of the neighborhood. Adjacent lots may be bare too.

Ponds For Ducks

If one is fortunate enough to have a pond or other water area on his property, plans for development may be entirely different from those described above for land birds. Included in the program may be such plants as sedges, rushes, and floating plants. Plans for water bird areas of various kinds are discussd in Chapter Six.

Other Considerations

Utilitarian considerations sometimes enter the picture. When a screen of trees is desired to hide an unsightly view, some of the plants can be selected with the bird's needs in mind.

Lastly, but by no means least, plantings serve to increase the sale value of a home.

The Back Yard (Concluded)

Among all bird habitats, the back yard holds the greatest potential for systematic study. The observer is there regularly, the birds are accustomed to the presence of people and act naturally, camera studies can be made of the birds, their songs can be wired into the house, phenological studies can be made, progress of migration can be monitored, and, as no salaried workers are involved, the observer can take his time. The interest of the landowner is perpetually kept alive, for he can never foretell what will happen next. He has a proprietary interest in all that takes place. Long may he reign!

Birds often fly against picture windows and similar surfaces, as though they were a part of the landscape, and are killed, but sheer coverings are now available that will lessen the damage to the victim. These may be attached to the outer window frame and stretched across the window. As the window frame extends outward slightly, there will be an air space between the window glass and the covering.

Many people enjoy putting out nesting materials for birds. Care should be exercised when making the selection however. Long pieces of string should not be used as the birds get tangled in it and may even hang themselves. In dry weather, mud can be provided, as certain species such as robins are dependent upon it. Occasionally birds start their nests in outbuildings or garages and later get shut out when their eggs need to be incubated. To keep the doors either open or closed throughout the nesting season would seem to be the logical answer to this problem.

Keep dogs under control during the nesting season as some species of birds nest on the ground.

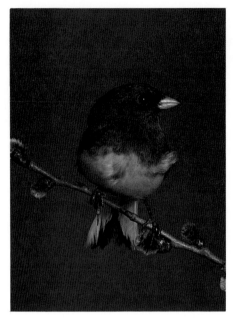

Dark-eyed Junco. *Junco hyemalis.* (male) The Dark-eyed Junco frequents our back yards, our roadsides, and our woodland edges. It seems to exude peace and contentment when it sings. Many people know it as the *snowbird.* When traveling, juncos take a leisurely pace. They occur in flocks, but travel from tree to tree a few birds at a time. (My picture was taken in Wisconsin.) 15 cm. (6")

Eastern Screech-Owl, *Otus asio.* Screech-Owls spend much of their time about towns and villages (if well-wooded) attracted perhaps by the flocks of House Sparrows that are usually present. People have been surprised, if not dumbfounded, occasionally, when they unwittingly approached the vicinity of the nest, and the parent bird swooped down upon their heads. 23 cm. (9")

Northern Mockingbird, *Mimus polyglottos.* The young mockingbird shown here has been out of the nest for only a short time. It has not yet had the opportunity to arrange its tail feathers. I have confidence, however, that it will escape from its enemies, for its parents are excellent fighters. I saw one of them alight on the back of a dog that was nearby, in an attempt to drive it away. 25 cm. (10″)

American Goldfinch, *Carduelis tristis.* (male) In winter, the males resemble the females, but they retain their light-yellow shoulder patch, a mark that the females do not have. 13 cm. (5″)

Field Trips

A friend of mine once told me that a certain committee, upon examining many years of field reports collected by a bird society, found that *most migratory birds arrived on weekends!* Today, because of the exisitng work week, I believe that most birders prefer to get out on weekends, but midweek field trips, taken either before or after work, are rewarding, as birds are active both early in the morning and late in the afternoon. Early morning is the best, though, as the birds sing more frequently and move about more during this period.

Most birders go out in the spring, no matter what happens. To get them out in the *fall* season is quite another matter. Authors of state bird books often have to guess at fall migration dates, due to this lack of enthusiasm for fall birdwatching.

I like to travel on trails as opposed to "plowing" through the brush. The latter method serves only to frighten the birds away. Wild mammal trails or cattle trails are useful where there are no brushed out lanes. In recent years, snowmobile trails have been a great help to hikers. Some birders like to hike alone, but I have never found the company of a few companions to be a handicap. On the contrary, extra pairs of eyes and ears are always helpful. Working on foot is much more productive than riding in a car. I believe everyone is agreed on this. (This is not to say that cars, boats, horses, and the like do not have their places. They do.)

Some Tricks of the Trade

If the weather is windy, it will pay to work on the leeward side of a hill or woods as the birds will be more plentiful there. When walking through habitat used by Ruffed Grouse and other species that habitually *sit tight,* always pause at short intervals. Such pauses, if quiet, will cause the birds to flush. Contrarywise, when surveying marsh habitat for rails or herons, pause at suitable intervals and make a sudden loud noise such as hand-clapping. This will cause the rails to call and herons to rise. Try for owls primarily on *clear* nights—they do not call as frequently on cloudy nights. It is possible to *call* many species of birds out into the open. (This is discussed in a separate section below.)

Conducting Field Trips (General)

I got my first taste of conducting field trips when I lived in St. Louis. The local bird club conducted field trips in certain city parks every spring. Many people came to participate, so they had to be divided into small groups. I found that most people were eager to learn. Because the groups were kept small, participants were able to see the birds. No effort was made to point out songs unless the singer could be seen, for songs in the abstract mean very little to beginners. In all of the groups, consisting mostly of adults, there were a few children. I did not find them to be a hinderance. Today, I can recognize some of those "children" within the ranks of our best ornithologists.

Those conducting the trips were cautioned to create a "feel" for the species in question—why it was found where it was, how it differed from its near relatives, and whether it had any peculiar mannerisms. To simply name the bird was not enough. For obvious reasons, we never took groups to occupied nests. The temptation to do this is ever present among leaders but it would set a bad example. Enemies, that never would have found it otherwise, are attracted to the nest because of the pandemonium created by the parent birds under such circumstances. Also, the parent birds themselves are more vulnerable to their enemies while

Common Snipe, *Gallinago gallinago.* In common with certain other species, the snipe tries to divert the attention of the intruder from its nest. The latter is often located on the ground, and in the vicinity of a marsh. The breeding range is broad, extending from the arctic regions, southward to the latitude of the Great Lakes, and even farther in the West. 28 cm. (11″)

Black-bellied Plover, *Pluvialis squatarola.* The Black-bellied Plover is circumpolar in distribution, but its nesting range with us (arctic tundra), extends from Baffin Island to western Alaska. Its upperparts are paler than those of the Lesser Golden Plover, with which the species can be confused. Ironically, the posterior portion of the belly of the subject species is white. 30 cm. (12″)

Flycatcher. When I took the picture of this flycatcher, the Willow Flycatcher and the Alder Flycatcher were combined under the name, *Traill's* Flycatcher, so I did not attempt to separate the species. Moreover, the picture was taken in the fall when the birds were not calling. (The bird shown here was simply yawning, believe it or not.) 14 cm. (5.5")

Northern Saw-whet Owl, *Aegolius acadicus.* Many years ago, this species was named *Saw-whet* because one of its calls sounds like the whetting or filing of a large saw. The bird is slightly smaller than a Screech-Owl, has yellow eyes and a dark bill, but no ear tufts. Young birds are more solidly colored and darker in appearance than the adults. 20 cm. (8")

bent on defending their nests. Further, the young may be frightened from their nests prematurely.

Conducting Field Trips At Conventions

Convention committees, in their early announcements, often play up unusual birds that will be seen on the convention tours. As a result of such publicity many guests spend considerable amounts of money to get to the conventions. I take it for granted, therefore, that the tour leaders will make every effort to produce the birds in question. The best tour leaders are not in every case, those who are the most knowledgeable, but rather those who beam with enthusiasm and are eager to serve.

Then, there is the problem of all, or almost all, guests signing up for the same tour, possibly one conducted by the most popular leader. The outcome of this is obvious—no one will see very much. To avoid this problem, it is best to dispense with the *signing up* routine and allow the people to gather in a large group, in a parking lot for example. The tour director, after surveying the size of the crowd, can then assign a leader to a certain portion, depending upon the number of leaders available. Of course, a few people may slip around behind the back of the director to switch leaders, but usually this is not a serious problem.

The Bird Census

Surveys of bird populations may be conducted in various ways. The following will serve as examples:

The Christmas Bird Count. The Christmas Bird Count, as conducted by the National Audubon Society, owes its beginning to Frank M. Chapman, a prominent ornithologist, while he was editor of *Bird-Lore.* It has grown into a very sizable undertaking today, and many people would not miss taking part in it for anything. Keen competition develops between rival groups and long hours are spent, but it is all in fun.

Areas covered in the count may include all bird habitats within a prescribed boundary, and any number of observers may participate. Some groups survey their appointed territories ahead of time in order to see what they will encounter. In the colder regions where I have helped with these counts, I find some of the best concentrations of birds near human habitation. Food supplies are often better here than elsewhere. Of course, this does not apply to all species of birds.

As the emphasis is usually on obtaining record numbers of species, the integrity of the observer is often severely tested. One friend of mine used to put it facetiously, "If you tell me what you need yet on the list, it will help my imagination." I am sure, however, that most observers try hard to be accurate.

The May Day Count. Usually this count is conducted during the *peak* of the spring migration. Thus it could fall before or after the month of May, depending upon the latitude. It is conducted similarly to the Christmas count, but it does not receive the same attention in our national magazines as the latter. Some participants count species only, as it is almost a hopeless task to count individuals during the spring migration. Competition among rival teams is high, and many observers work longer than eighteen hours on this day.

The Breeding Bird Survey. This survey differs in several ways from the others I have discussed. Under the supervision of the United States Migratory Bird and Habitat Research Laboratory, Laurel, Maryland, it was set up in 1966 to obtain information annually on our bird populations during the nesting season. As the work is done under the direct supervision of the above-

Tricolored Heron, *Egretta tricolor.* Three colors stand out in the plumage of this species, so it is now called the Tricolored Heron. Formerly, it was known as the Louisiana Heron. It is slender in appearance and about the size of the Little Blue Heron. When feeding, it may either wait for its prey to approach, or actively pursue it. 66 cm. (26")

Turkey Vulture and Black Vulture. I took this picture to show the difference in size of two of our vultures. The Turkey Vulture is on the right. I tried to photograph a California Condor one day as it flew overhead, but it was too quick for me. I wanted to show how large it was when compared with the other vultures.

Kentucky Warbler, *Oporornis formosus.* The Kentucky Warbler, a ground species, nests by choice in deciduous forests that have a dense understory. It is not limited in its range to one state, but was named for Kentucky by Wilson when he found it to be common there. The best time to see the male is while he is singing, for then, he is most likely to be off the ground. 14cm. (5.5″)

Red-eyed Vireo, *Vireo olivaceus.* I obtained this picture near the end of September, in Wisconsin. The bird did not call, but judging by its appearance, it must be an immature Red-eyed Vireo. 15cm. (6″)

named agency, it is best for prospective participants to contact that office. In general, certain prescribed routes are run by car, with stops every half-mile (.80 km.) and within a designated time period. Much reliance is placed upon bird sounds, so the observer must be more than a beginner. Only one or two observers are needed to run a given route.

Thorough Search Of A Small Tract. Surveys of small tracts of land may be conducted in various ways and during almost any season of the year. If an estimate of populations is desired, at least eight or ten visits during the appropriate season may be needed. If only the species composition is wanted, a few less surveys will suffice.

Value Of The Surveys

Surveys such as the Christmas Bird Count and the Breeding Bird Survey serve to show trends in populations—whether up or down. Best results are obtained when these surveys are conducted in the same way each year and by the same personnel. Thorough searches of small tracts, when conducted systematically, probably give us the best information on numbers. All types of surveys, including the May Day Counts, help to show the seasonal distribution of birds.

Calling Birds

There are a number of ways to call birds into the open for easy identification. Some of the sounds to be produced are designed to imitate the calls of the bird in question, while others imitate creatures in distress. Before mechanical devices were invented ornithologists made sounds to imitate creatures in distress by vigorously kissing the back of the hand. Another method was to make a sort of "gushing" hiss. I call this the "schwe-bee" sound.

Today, mechanical squeekers are available on the market. The most important innovation though, is the tape recorder. The system in use is to record a bird's call or song and then play it back to it. In many cases this will bring the bird out into the open. Another way is to play back the sounds of creatures in distress. Recorders are available to almost anyone, and to use them to call birds is generally a harmless pastime, but to repeatedly call out a bird, particularly one of a rare species, can be detrimental, for in the latter case, "everybody" wants to get a look. Caution is the watchword also when eggs or nestlings are present, for to call out the parent birds at this time may serve to alert an enemy. Not all birds respond to our efforts to call them. Those that do may do so for only a short time, particularly during the nonbreeding season.

Identification

Some time ago when I was in Colorado, I stopped for supplies at a small store. A porchlike shelter covered the front entrance, and under this structure a Say's Phoebe had nested. "How long has that bird been around here," I asked. "That *thrush* comes every year," the store keeper replied. Well, we do not expect everyone to be an authority. We do expect those who conduct field trips to know the birds, however.

Not so long ago, I observed some men taking a census of birds around a small lake. A Yellow-throated Vireo rendered one of its explosive calls (not its song). Down on the list went a Sora (rail). The men had associated the sound with the habitat before them and assumed that the bird in question must be a rail. I did not have the heart to correct them on the spot.

Consulting the books beforehand is a commendable habit, but it is not the complete answer. Recently, a man

Yellow-throated Vireo, *Vireo flavifrons.* Contrary to the ways of some of our vireos, this species spends much of its time in the treetops—often of the deciduous type—and here, it builds its nest, the male assisting the female. Its song can be heard from a distance, though, as it is unusually loud. 14 cm. (5.5″)

Double-crested Cormorant, *Phalacrocorax auritus.* My illustration demonstrates that a swimming cormorant may not show very much of its body. The bird can be recognized, though, by the tilt of its head, the bill pointing upward. (The two crests are not very conspicuous.) This species has the widest distribution of all our cormorants, and is probably the best-known. 84 cm. (33″)

Willet, *Catoptrophorus semipalmatus.* The prominently-striped wings and the persistent *pill-o-will-o-willet* call combine to make identification of the Willet a simple matter when it is in flight. When at rest, though, the bird may appear to be uniformly grayish-brown. 38cm. (15″)

Dunlin, *Calidris alpina.* This species might well have been named the *Black-bellied Sandpiper,* for its dark belly stands out prominently against its pale underparts in summer plumage. My photograph was taken in Texas during April, so the plumage is not yet at its best. The bird standing in the center foreground is a Sanderling. 20cm. (8″)

showed me a bird sitting on the ground in the *posture* of a Horned Lark which he had seen in a bird book. He was certain it must be a Horned Lark. Well, it was a House Sparrow in an environment entirely unsuited to Horned Larks. What then is the answer?

To try to identify the sex of a bird, when this is possible by color, is one way to assure greater accuracy. Another way is to write detailed notes on the spot which can be analyzed later with the help of books. That the plumage of birds may change with the seasons or with the age of the birds is well-known. What may not always be taken into account is how the variability of light may affect one's accuracy of vision. Further, white birds such as swans may have stained plumage. To identify a few birds of a flock and assume that the entire flock is made up of the same species is a common fallacy. Whenever a nest or eggs are found, it is advisable to wait for the birds to show up for accurate identification purposes. The nests and eggs of many species vary considerably, depending upon a number of factors.

Many editors of field note publications require documentation of all rare species. In addition to details on the bird itself, they like to have supporting evidence such as how close the observer was to the bird, the power of the binocular used, the light conditions, and the names of companions, if any. Regarding the bird itself, a long list of helpful details can be drawn up, but the principal ones are size, family characteristics such as shape and actions, color, song or calls, habitat, season, and what kinds of birds were with it.

List Chasers

The sound of this heading raises eyebrows in some circles. Some people consider list chasing to be a frivolous side of the hobby of bird study, and yet it has its useful side. It gets people out more often than they would otherwise go; those who do it acquire experience in bird identification, and very often, it leads to more valuable pursuits.

Dyed-in-the-wool list chasers travel far and wide to enlarge their life lists. Some participants have seen most of the species indigenous to our land. Competition is keen among the contestants, and records are kept as to who is in the lead.

The organization that caters to travelers in this category is the American Birding Association. In recent years, this association has been concerned about the image of birders in the eyes of the public. In their eagerness to add another species, a few list-chasers have made the headlines in the news—headlines that were unfavorable because they disregarded the rights of other people, and also because they subjected the birds in question to unnecessary danger.

Field Trip Equipment

If a birder strapped on all of the equipment useful on field trips, he would look like a salesman. When I go on foot, I travel as lightly as possible. If I need a lunch, I carry only a sandwich. My winter clothing is warm but light weight. I wear gym shoes as they cling well to most surfaces. In short, I try to be comfortable.

Lightweight binoculars are ample for most purposes. The 7 x 35 models are the preferred combination. Coated optics are better than uncoated as they admit more light. Center focus is the most convenient, and special eyepieces are available to those who wear glasses.

In addition to the binocular, many observers keep a spotting scope handy for long-distance viewing. Magnification up to thirty times is feasible for bird observation.

Royal Tern, *Sterna maxima.* This species and the Caspian Tern resemble each other closely, but there are a few marks to be noted. In the Royal Tern, the bill is orange (not red), the forehead is white except during the nesting season, the wingtips are paler on the underside, and the tail is more deeply-forked. 51cm. (20")

Least Tern, *Sterna antillarum.* This little tern is similar in size to the more widely distributed Black Tern. Perhaps its small size is in its favor, for it has maintained its numbers quite well. It is primarily a bird of the coastal beaches, although a fairly large population lives along our rivers in the lower Midwest. 23cm. (9")

Rusty Blackbird, *Euphagus carolinus.* (male) Rusty Blackbirds are so-named because their plumage in winter is more or less tinged with brown. This applies to the birds at this time regardless of their age or sex. In the spring, the rusty appearance disappears and the males take on their glossy black plumage, and the females their slaty-black garb. (I obtained my photograph in early spring.) 23 cm. (9″)

Lincoln's Sparrow, *Melospiza lincolnii.* Contrary to what we might expect, the subject species was not named for Abraham Lincoln, but for Thomas Lincoln, a friend of Audubon's. The bird does not make itself conspicuous, but the buffy band across its breast is an aid to identification. It does not sing very often during migration. 14 cm. (5.5″)

Stronger lenses are not satisfactory for terrestrial work in summer because of the heat waves. Usually a tripod or other device is used to steady the scope.

I mentioned the notebook and pencil above; many observers add a bird guide. Tape recorders and cameras are useful too. I shall have more to say about these items later.

Keeping Notebooks

Most ornithologists I have known keep records. The system used may be a loose-leaf notebook, a card file, or field cards. The system I like best permits daily notes to be entered by date and location in one book, while the same notes are entered by species in another book. If entries are made immediately in both books, the record will be accurate and available at any time.

Field notes that are of general interest readily find their way into bird magazines. *American Birds*, a publication of the National Audubon Society, makes, in my opinion, the most thorough digest of such notes. Publications of local or regional organizations also devote considerable space to field notes.

Notes may be kept on almost any aspect of ornithology, as it is difficult to predict what will be of interest. Migration dates and records of rarities are the easiest to obtain, but notes on the relative abundance of common species, nesting data, special life-history studies, phenological records, and night observations are of value.

Organization Work

Early in my career, I moved to a locality where there was neither a city nor a statewide bird club. I thought it would be nice to have one of each kind, so I wrote a letter to the personnel of a national organization to see if they could supply me with any help. They wrote that they had no help to offer, and furthermore, organizations of this kind usually sprang up of their own volition. As I did not quite agree with the latter part of this reply, I went at once to the local newspaper with the announcement that I would conduct a field trip for birders in one of the city parks next Sunday morning. (In those days, most people worked on Saturday.) The response was so encouraging that I did the same thing in other city parks on the following Sundays. Soon we had our city club organized. Meetings were held in the vocational school. Soon thereafter, this organization served as the spearhead for a statewide bird club.

When I lived in the St. Louis area, I belonged to a Nature Club, the members of which often met in groups, depending upon their special interests. Thus we had group sessions on birds, mammals, insects, wild flowers, and whatever else was pertinent. At other times, we had programs for members of the entire club. I enjoyed this system very much as fellow members could help one another on subjects in almost any field. Membership was open to anyone interested.

In other parts of the country, I have seen bird clubs that accepted members only by election. This means that candidates for membership must have a more or less professional status in the field. Also I have seen clubs that accepted almost anyone into its general membership, but at the same time had higher categories to which qualified persons could be elected.

Some clubs limit their interests to birds only; others include almost everything in the environmental field. Some run independently; others become chapters of a larger organization. In some cities, there may be more than one kind of bird club. It depends upon the local needs.

Great Blue Heron, *Ardea herodias.* Today this white heron is known as a form of the above named species. Its range is much smaller, however. It nests primarily in the area from southern Florida, through parts of the West Indies, to northern South America. (I took my photograph in southern Florida.) 119cm. (47″)

Black-necked Stilt, *Himantopus mexicanus.* The small flock of stilts shown here reminds us that the species is colonial in habits and feeds in shallow water. Stilts are able to swim or stand in deep water, but their food items, which include water insects, snails, and small fish, apparently may be gathered most easily in shallow water. 35cm. (14″)

Semi-palmated Plover, *Charadrius semipalmatus.* This plover resembles the much larger Killdeer in general color and pattern, but it lacks the orange rump of the latter, and wears only one black ring around its neck. It is called *semi-palmated* because its toes are partly-webbed. In common with other plovers, this species carries its head high and in this way differs in profile from most of our sandpipers. 18cm. (7")

Pectoral Sandpiper, *Calidris melanotos.* I took this picture during late summer. The bird had just mounted the higher ground to rest after taking a swim in the nearby water. Its colors had not changed greatly from those worn during the breeding season. Most of our birds breed in the arctic regions, but they migrate in numbers to South America. 23cm. (9")

Getting Started

I take it for granted that all clubs will draw up a constitution. In this connection, it is usually advisable to incorporate the organization, for problems associated with large sums of money or property eventually will arise. Obtaining a special "nonprofit organization" mailing permit is vital, as it not only reduces mailing costs, it may enable doners to use their club donations as deductions on their income tax report. I am here referring to generous donations which often are made to conservation causes. Unless an organization is incorporated, it is in a weak position to accept endowments, buy land, or do anything else on a large scale. Another precaution is to number the meetings that are held. There are several reasons why this is useful, but one of the most important is to guard against fraud. The minutes of a certain meeting could be conveniently lost.

In order to start an organization or build it up, it is essential, first of all, that the leader or leaders be dedicated to the cause. Hard work will be required and not all of one's efforts will be rewarded. Favorable publicity is always a great help, and the best way to obtain news coverage is to do something really worthy of attention.

Displays in public places often help to gain members, and these could consist of art objects such as paintings, carved birds, habitat demonstrations, or anything that comes to mind. If possible, it is a good idea to give *all* members a job. All members will bring guests, and there will be a "hand shaker" at the door to make everyone feel at ease.

Much To Be Done

It has been said that a conference is comprised of a group of people discussing what they *should be doing.*

Well, there are many things to be done.

Local clubs can arrange, in addition to their indoor meetings, field trips, including camping, and safaris to distant places. They can send young people to Nature study camps by means of scholarships. Clubs can engage speakers of national prominence to present movies or programs for the benefit of the public. Such performances often are held in large school auditoriums or other public buildings, and admission tickets are sold in advance as well as at the door to cover the costs. Nature trails are popular today, and often they can be set up and maintained by a local club. Perhaps it is possible even to purchase and develop a bird sanctuary for such a purpose.

In regular meetings it is desirable, in addition to the featured program, to receive verbal reports of local bird observations from everyone present. Discussion of such reports can become the "lifeblood" of the club. It is helpful if the club can have printed a field card on which the birds that are to be expected in the vicinity are listed.

Frequently, governmental agencies concerned with birds can be called upon for speakers and other help. It is understood that local club members will acquaint themselves with the activities of all governmental agencies concerned with birds and cooperate with them wherever possible. Mutual help and concern is a great thing.

If cooperation is desired from the public for a bird club project, usually it can be obtained if the public is informed of the need in the right way. Thus favorable connections should be maintained with the news agencies at all times.

Gray Kingbird, *Tyrannus dominicensis.* This kingbird, a subtropical species, nests in the Florida Keys and the adjacent mainland of southern Florida. (I obtained my photograph in the latter area.) It spends the winters in the West Indies or in northern South America, so we do not expect it until late March or early April. 23 cm. (9")

Nest of Altamira Oriole, *Icterus gularis.* I was able to photograph this nest while visiting the Santa Ana National Wildlife Refuge during April. It was located high in a tree, and appeared to be about 61 cm. (2 ft.) in the vertical dimension. Until recently, the subject species was known as *Lichtenstein's Oriole.* It is fairly common in Mexico, but barely reaches the United States.

Boat-tailed Grackle, *Quiscalus major.* Whenever I hear one of these grackles vocalize, I am reminded of my elementary school days when, if you pinched the boy ahead of you, he would let out a sudden shriek. Judging by the way the male in the accompanying picture is perched, it seems that someone pinched him. The female is smaller than the male, and, as can be seen in the photograph, she is brownish in color. She builds her nest in trees and other vegetation, sometimes over water. Except in Florida where the birds may be found inland, the species is mostly coastal in distribution. I photographed the pair in their nest tree, which was located in Fort Lauderdale, Florida. It was during the month of April. Male 41 cm. (16″), female 33 cm. (13″)

Maintaining A Store

State-wide or province-wide bird clubs can do things on a broader scale than can be expected of local clubs. One thing that can be done better is to maintain a "store." I had the dubious honor of starting such an enterprise. After running it for a while, I found that I was between two "fires." On one hand, to hold my customers, I had to build up the inventory, thereby depleting my profits. On the other hand, if I turned over any cash to the club, I could not buy enough merchandise. In short, the progress of this type of enterprise is slow, but once it gets over the "hump" it is a rewarding feature.

As in any business, there is a lot of work connected with the store. Perhaps the best solution to this problem is to set up a committee of at least two or three people who are willing to share the responsibilities.

The best time to sell merchandise is at meetings such as annual conventions. The variety of things of interest to birders on the market today is tremendous, and at such meetings, the people will become acquainted with the merchandise. Everyone, of course, will have the opportunity to order by mail at any time.

Income earned by the store will be tax free if the club spends it on the proper things. (This can best be checked out locally. Excise tax and state tax must be paid where it applies, however.) A good bookkeeping system is imperative.

It is possible to obtain merchandise in small quantities from wholesalers today, and if credit is needed, it usually can be arranged. As the volume of sales increases larger quantities of merchandise can be ordered at one time to save on shipping charges and to take advantage of quantity discounts. Official club stationary and forms should be prepared in advance for use in all business transactions.

In order to obtain a variety of merchandise it is necessary to deal with a large number of wholesalers. This may not be feasible at first, so the store manager may decide, as a temporary expedient, to deal with a few distributors, although the margin of profit will be less. Addresses of wholesalers (including book publishers) and distributors are available in most large libraries.

The store manager is in an excellent position to conduct "white elephant" sales periodically. Unwanted articles contributed by club members usually can be sold at one hundred percent profit.

All club publications, such as local bird check lists, can be handled by the store. The store manager may be in position to give the club magazine editor a boost. One of the companies from which he purchases a quantity of merchandise may be willing to cooperate with reference to color printing for the magazine, perhaps for an anniversary issue. (This is assuming that the club cannot afford to pay for color.) For example, a stationery company that specializes in printing birds in color might be persuaded to run off some cover stock— enough for one issue of the magazine—in exchange for a full page add on the back of the magazine. I had good luck with this plan.

The store manager should have voting power in all financial matters of the club. Otherwise, someone not acquainted with the problems of the store manager could easily offset his gains.

Convention Speakers

Annual conventions are rather costly and the tendency on the part of the planning committee often is to refrain from engaging well-known speakers. In my experience, this can turn out to be false economy.

Black Skimmer, *Rynchops niger.* Black Skimmers make a beautiful picture when in flight. It is not unusual to see such pictures, for the birds are strongly gregarious. Even during the breeding season, this trait stands out, for they place their nests so close together that the incubating birds can scarcely rise from their eggs without disturbing their neighbors. 46 cm. (18")

Sandwich Tern, *Sterna sandvicensis.* The Sandwich Tern could be confused with such species as the Common Tern, were it not for the color of its bill. The subject species is our only regular tern having a black bill with a yellow tip. (Immatures, of course, may not show the tip clearly.) The species was named for the place where it was first collected. 38 cm. (15")

Green Jay, *Cyanocorax yncas.* This colorful jay ranges from the central part of South America, northward through many parts of Mexico. It crosses the Rio Grande in the vicinity of the Santa Ana National Wildlife Refuge, but does not go very far northward into Texas. It favors the wooded lowlands. (I took my picture in the refuge.) 28 cm. (11″)

Scissor-tailed Flycatcher, *Tyrannus forficatus.* I believe it is the ambition of every ornithologist to see this flycatcher in its native habitat. Truly it is one of our most spectacular birds. Not only is it something to see for its color, its actions are amazing. The long tail, of course, contributes to the latter. (I obtained my picture in Texas.) 35 cm. (14″)

Frequently a national "figure" will bring in more extra revenue than is required to pay his expenses. The side effects of this are valuable too, as regular members and visitors will come out in greater numbers in succeeding years, realizing that the program will be truly worthwhile.

Club Publications

If a magazine or newsletter is started, one way to create interest in it is to conduct a contest for a suitable name.

It may be desirable to have two kinds of publications: a newsletter for the more urgent matters and a magazine issued at suitable intervals for articles of a permanent nature. The latter can be exchanged with magazines in other parts of the country.

In most magazines there is a section devoted to field notes. Here, two problems present themselves which I would like to discuss. First, there is the problem of the reliability of field notes. When I was editor of a magazine many years ago, an individual whom I had never met reported a small flock of Worming-eating Warblers in an area somewhat to the north of their usual range, and in April, which was early at best. I knew what was wrong, but I did not tell him bluntly. Instead, I wrote him a nice letter explaining the status of the Worm-eating Warbler and asked if he had considered the Golden-crowned Kinglet. He replied at once, stating that the birds in question were indeed Golden-crowned Kinglets and thanked me profusely for getting him on the right track.

Not all cases are as simple as this. What should one do, for example, if a friend insists that he has seen "such and such" which is well nigh impossible? Some observers *do,* in fact, *see* precisely *that.* On the other hand, what becomes of the integrity of a publication if it is filled with unusual records? Assuredly, the editor will not publish them and say in print that certain observers must have been mistaken!

Secondly, there is the problem of forms on which field notes are to be submitted. Of course, one can eliminate forms completely and take what comes in, perhaps with a few general instructions, but this system eventually will bring in such a mass of data that the editor, who has to make the final report, will be bogged down with detail. If forms are used, it is imperative that they be kept simple. The average business person today simply does not have the time to analyze an intricate system. Better to miss getting certain details, and get instead the more important records from a large number of observers, including probably the best ornithologists.

Incidentally, field notes are valuable. Most of them will be useful to the author of the state or provincial bird book. If a book of this kind has already been published, no doubt, it will have to be revised at some future time.

Book Reviews

Book reviews frequently are included in club magazines. Recently, I read a book review written by a nationally-known writer that was negative in the extreme. Simultaneously, the same organization that published this review came out in another branch of its literature with an appraisal of the same book, written in words of highest praise, by an internationally-known ornithologist. From this, I am reminded that not all authorities look at a book in the same way. By the same token, we could say that no two authors will write a book on a given subject in the same way. Moreover, incidental problems such as tight budgets sometimes force publishers to cut "corners." It seems, therefore, that the book reviewer should describe both the good and the bad points about the

Plain Chachalaca, *Ortalis vetula.* This slender species of Mexico and Central America, enters the United States along the lower Rio Grande, in Texas. It is adept at hiding in the forests and thickets that make up its habitat, but when it calls, it leaves no doubt as to its whereabouts. (I took my picture in the Santa Ana National Wildlife Refuge.) 56 cm. (22″)

Wood Stork, *Mycteria americana.* The Wood Stork, formerly known as the Wood Ibis, is a beautiful bird in flight. It spends much of its time flying in circles over its nesting area. At close range, it is not quite so beautiful, for its head and upper neck is bare and dark in color. Its large bill is a help in identification. 102 cm. (40″)

Laughing Gull, *Larus atricilla.* If the northern bird observer ever wondered why this species is called the Laughing Gull, he will find out on his first visit to the Gulf Coast. The first gull to greet him, very likely will be one of this species, and if it has never seen a northern bird observer before, it may express its opinion of him verbally. 43 cm. (17")

Anhinga, *Anhinga anhinga.* (male) This species has been known by such names as snakebird, darter, or water turkey. When swimming, it often shows only its snake-like head and neck; when feeding, it thrusts its long, sharp bill forward like a dart; and when flying, it spreads its tail somewhat in turkey-fashion, but the latter name (allusion) is not as fitting as the other two. 89 cm. (35")

book under consideration as this would allow the prospective buyer to make his own decision, without fear of bias. The most constructive manner in which to handle glowing errors is to contact the author privately. He, in turn, can have the publisher print an errata sheet and insert it in the preface of subsequent copies.

Telephone Alert

Some organizations maintain a telephone "alert" system, the main purpose of which is to enable interested observers to obtain a look at rare birds before they move on. Anyone observing a species of interest may call in the message, including the location where seen and the date. The system works automatically once it has been installed. Of course, there is some expense involved.

Keeping The Organization Alive

All bird organizations are subject to decline after a number of years. If the original founders pass out of the picture this, in itself, may signal the demise. It is important that the organization try to maintain a good public image. Is it always against something? Does it have trouble keeping its members? Do certain persons wield too much influence? These are all signs of decline.

A bird club can be fun. It can be helpful in many ways to the community. Long may it live!

National and International Organizations

Many organizations exist today that are of interest to ornithologists. The following are examples: American Birding Association, The American Ornithologists' Union, Bird-Banding Associations (regional), The Colonial Waterbird Group, The Cooper Ornithological Society, The Ecological Society of America, Hawk Mountain Sanctuary

Association, International Council for Bird Preservation, International Crane Foundation, National Audubon Society, National Wildlife Federation, The Nature Conservancy, Neotropical Ornithological Society, North American Bluebird Society, Ottawa Field-Naturalists' Club, The Pacific Seabird Group, The Raptor Research Foundation, Society of Canadian Ornithologists, Western Field Ornithologists, The Wilderness Society, Wildlife Management Institute, The Wildlife Society, The Wilson Ornithological Society, World Wildlife Fund—United States.

No preferential treatment is meant here. There are many more that could be mentioned, including the various governmental agencies.

Traveling to See New Birds

This is the age of bird safaris. It is possible today to take part in organized tours throughout most parts of the world.

Bird Song Recordings

Bird song recordings serve many purposes. As mentioned previously, they serve to bring birds out into the open where they can be studied and identified. Similarly, they serve to bring birds out into view where they can be photographed. I shall have more to say on this later.

Song recordings have demonstrated that very few birds ever sing the same song in *precisely* the same way. And yet these songs are recognizable. The birds also recognize them as can be seen when they drive away their competitors. An interesting sidelight to me is the fact birds do not, as a rule, attack the Northern Mockingbird when it imitates their songs.

One day while attempting to photograph a male

Roseate Spoonbill, *Ajaia ajaia.* I took this picture in April, so the birds were through nesting. (They begin nesting activities during the winter.) I was impressed by their color and by their liking for one another. They even work together while searching for food. Included in the diet are small fish, mollusks, slugs, and insects. 79 cm. (31″)

Double-crested Cormorant, *Phalacrocorax auritus.* Here we see two plumages of the cormorant, the one on the left being the immature. Many people call the adults sea crows because they are so dark in color. They perch upright as a rule. It is interesting to note that wildlife managers are now building nest platforms in trees to aid this species. 84 cm. (33″)

Least Grebe, *Tachybaptus dominicus.* This tropical species ranges year-round as far north as southern Texas and rarely elsewhere north of the Rio Grande, but it is difficult to detect because of its small size and diving habits. (I obtained my photograph in the Santa Ana National Wildlife Refuge.) 25 cm. (10″)

Herring Gull, *Larus argentatus.* The Herring Gull ranges throughout most of North America, so it is one of our best-known species. It is not considered to be a pest, as it feeds on a great variety of foods; in fact, it is often thought of as a scavenger. It ranges also in the Old World. (The bird pictured is in immature plumage.) 61 cm. (24″)

Marsh Wren (formerly Long-billed Marsh Wren), I played back the bird's *own* song. No sooner had he heard it when he flew for my recorder. He flew for it repeatedly, thus indicating that he meant business.

To record bird songs for the uses outlined above is easy, and little patience is required. To make recordings that can be used in the lecture hall is quite another matter. I never knew, for example, that there were so many airplanes until I started to make bird song recordings! Equipment that is sensitive enough to record bird songs will pick up motor sounds from afar. Farm marchinery and highway traffic also become a hinderance. When is the best time to record songs, then? Perhaps the early morning hours afford the best opportunity. Fortunately, strong winds, which are also a great hinderance, are often weak at this time.

To get away from the loud calls of blackbirds, presents a challenge. And when the operator believes he has finally approached the singer closely enough for recording purposes, the bird stops singing. So, if and when a flawless recording is obtained, there is cause for rejoicing.

Bird Photography

One day, while I was photographing birds in California and using my car as a blind, a man drove up behind me and parked without my knowledge. I was waiting for a Western Sandpiper to come within range. At about the time the sandpiper was in the right place, this man shouted, "Now!" Well, I believe that sandpiper must be still flying from fright!

I always knew that some people could make themselves nuisances around camera blinds, but I never thought that birds would. A Ring-billed Gull I photographed recently, must be an exception, for he appeared to be getting a belly laugh after frightening away two terns I was trying to include in the picture.

It is now comparatively easy to photograph birds, as cameras and other equipment have been improved, and film better adapted. If a person is interested in photographing birds in flight, he can obtain a gunstock to help steady the camera. If there are doubts about lighting conditions or distance, a separate camera, and film which can be developed at once, can be used for quick verification. Excellent magnification is obtainable in telephoto lenses, and pictures can be taken when birds are brought out into the open by means of tape recorders.

It is possible to obtain good photographs in places where birds are regularly fed, in refuges that serve to concentrate them, and from roads that run through their habitats.

Despite these advantages, it still is difficult to obtain excellent results. The bird may move at the last moment, the camera might fail at the most crucial time, or the pose obtained may not be typical of the species. If the photographer is working at a nest, the birds may refuse to return; and when birds in the sun notice that they are being watched, they usually flee to the shade. Considerable time, patience, and expense is involved. Nevertheless, when a few good pictures are obtained, it seems that most of the troubles fade away.

Bluebird House Trails

Bluebird house trails, made popular by T.E. Musselman during the early 1930's, serve a useful purpose. Indeed, I have found them to be of considerable value. The bluebird (eastern species in particular) is vulnerable to extremely cold temperatures, suffers from competition with European Starlings and House Sparrows, and

Ruby-throated Hummingbird, *Archilochus colubris.* (female) Normally, when hummingbirds fly, they keep their wings in constant motion. Thus I would like to include this photograph to show what the wings look like. I have a second reason, too. It seems from the appearance of the right eye, that the bird is plagued with mites. This is a common malady among birds as they are not able to scratch them out of the area of the eyes. 9cm. (3.5")

The Gull Gets A Laugh. The terns flew away before I had a chance to identify them, but they appear to be Common Terns.

Rufous-sided Towhee, *Pipilo erythrophthalmus.* (male) Not all the towhees combined under the above name are similar in appearance. When in Florida, I saw a form that had white eyes; and when in California, I saw a form that showed an abundance of white in the wings. The latter has some distinctive calls too. In the Midwest, we describe the typical song by the phrase, *see-tow-hee-e-e.* (Photograph was taken in Wisconsin.) 20cm. (8")

Common Yellowthroat, *Geothlypis trichas.* I photographed this young male in Wisconsin during September. Apparently it is a bird of the year. 13cm. (5")

lacks good nesting sites in general. Bluebird house trails have been set up primarily for the eastern species to date, but all species of bluebirds can use them with profit. A favorable side effect is that swallows, titmice, wrens, and other cavity-nesters get a chance to use some of them. I am assuming, of course, that there will be a surplus of houses.

It is a good idea to obtain the permission of the landowner before putting up houses on his property. I prefer to locate them in the hinterlands whenever possible, as dangers inherent along roads often offset the gains. If they can be kept at a considerable distance from farm buildings, there will be less interference by House Sparrows and cats. If cattle use the area, the houses should be mounted above their reach, or if on fence posts, they should be kept to the opposite side of the fence. Cattle like to scratch themselves on such projections and will knock them down. Bluebirds like to have their houses in the open, as on fence posts, although this is not an absolute rule. Orchard-type woodlands are satisfactory, but I would not place them in the vicinity of orchards as these are sprayed, and insect food found there may be poisonous. There is no value in spacing the houses closer than about 137 meters (150 yards), as male bluebirds are competitive. If they can be located in areas where at least a part of the habitat is devoted to short grass (such as pastures and lawns), they stand the best chance of being occupied, because the birds pick up much of their food from the ground.

When houses are painted in conspicuous colors, I have found that they make good targets for trigger-happy gunners. Also, they invite frequent inspection by the public. To discourage the latter, I secure the roof boards with one or two wood screws. I do not nail them as I must inspect the houses periodically for House Sparrow nests and other nuisances, and the houses need to be cleaned out at least once a year. Needless to say, with all the work involved, it is poor economy to construct the houses of any material other than the strongest. This is especially true in bear country. I discourage the use of tin cans and plastic bottles and do not recommend glass roofs, as curiosity seekers are not wanted.

Several methods have been tried to discourage "long-armed" mammals such as cats or raccoons. One of the best is to build the houses tall so that the entrance door can be located high above the nest. This method not only discourages the mammals, it forces the young birds to remain in the nest a day or two longer than otherwise, thereby aiding their survival. It seems also that the cowbird is less likely to enter a deep box than one that is shallow. When the houses are mounted they may tilt forward a little when necessary, but never backward.

Another method to discourage mammalian predators is to hang the houses from a wire, stretched tightly between two posts or between two trees. In order for this to be effective the wire must be strong and able to hold the house well above the ground, above the reach of mammals that jump.

About the time the bluebirds return from their winter quarters, I find that my houses are filled with white-footed mice. Those houses that were occupied by House Wrens, if the mice failed to find them, are unsuitable for bluebirds as wrens fill them to the level of the entrance. (The bluebird's nest is a rather flat structure placed upon the bottom of the house.) Due to these possibilities bluebird houses should be checked and cleaned out shortly before the bluebirds are ready

Eastern Bluebird, *Sialia, sialis.* (male) Bluebirds are easy to find when they are present as they perch on utility wires and fence posts where they can be seen. From these perches, they fly down to the ground to pick up an insect or worm that they spy from above. Often they confine themselves to areas where the grass or other vegetation has been mowed. 18 cm. (7″)

Bluebird House. This is a typical situation for bluebirds. The grass is short enough to allow the birds to find their food, much of which is in or on the ground, and the birds can perch in the trees along the edge of the forest.

Tree Swallow, *Tachycineta bicolor.* Tree Swallows have benefited from bird house trails, operated in recent years for bluebirds. Actually, trails could be set up for the swallows alone as they have need for them. European Starlings and House Sparrows are making the birds unfair competition. Houses put up specifically for Tree Swallows serve best, of course, when located near water. 15 cm. (6″)

Tree Swallow, *Tachycineta bicolor.* My photograph illustrates the immature Tree Swallow. It was taken in June, shortly after the bird had left its nest, which, incidentally, was in one of my bluebird houses. It will join its fellows late in summer. We always see large flocks of them on the utility wires before they start southward. 15 cm. (6″)

to occupy them.

It may be neccessary or desirable to move some of the houses during the course of the nesting season. If for example, a snake is known to have visited a house, it is likely to return again.

The establishment and maintenance of a bluebird house trail requires the supervision of a mature person. It is not a project to be lightly undertaken, but, properly handled, it can be a great help to the birds. Bear in mind that we usrp a bird's prerogative of nest-site selection when we put up a house. If we make a poor selection, the season will be lost for them. Inspection by the operator can, in itself, be a hinderance as predators often follow in the footsteps of another creature. To open the house when the bird is inside can also be damaging.

Realizing that the creation and maintenance of a bluebird house trail is a specialized undertaking, a group of dedicated workers founded the North American Bluebird Society during the late 1970's. In 1984, this society received 6,000 responses from members of the National Wildlife Federation who read about the plight of the bluebird in the April issue of *National Wildlife.*

Two species of bluebirds (Eastern and Western) can use the same set of house specifications: *Floor inside*— 11 x 11 cm. (4½ x 4½ in.), *Entrance diameter*—3.8 cm. (1½ in.), *Entrance above floor*—20 cm. (8 in.), *Habitat*—open; scattered trees, *Above ground*—1.5 to 3 m. (5 to 10 feet). The Mountain Bluebird is slightly larger than the other two species, so the *floor inside* should be 13 x 13 cm. (5 x 5 in.), and the *entrance* diameter 4.1 cm. (1⅝ inch). Perches below the entrance attract House Sparrows, so they should be left off. If a person cannot build his own houses, he can purchase them on the market. He should check the specifications, though, to see that they meet fairly closely those spelled out above, particularly with reference to height of entrance above the floor.

Bird Carving

Bird carving has come into its own. I am here referring to models carved out of wood. If the birds are made according to scale and colored accurately, they make a useful and attractive display. It is necessary to select wood that is soft enough to carve yet hard enough to hold together. Pine is often used.

Bird-Banding

Bird-banding and other methods of marking birds are under the supervision of governmental agencies. Permits are required, and rules for the work are meticulously spelled out. A bird band is a sort of ring or bracelet which can be easily attached to the bird's tarsus (commonly called leg). On this band is a serial number and the name and address of the agency to whom recovery information should be sent. Coloring of a bird's feathers, colored streamers, and certain other markings are sometimes authorized for special studies.

In the past, much valuable service has been rendered in this field by amateur ornithologists. This is true today, although professionals are entering the picture at a rapid pace. One of the most discouraging features about the system is the low return. Very few bands are found by the public, and some people who find them misunderstand their purpose and are afraid to send them in. Yet, over the years, much has been learned about the birds through banding and marking.

If a band is found, the following procedure should be followed: Flatten out the band and tape it to a piece of note paper, or if this is impractical, copy the *complete* legend, including the numbers, from the band. Always

Eastern Bluebird, *Sialia sialis.* (female) The families of this species stay together in an admirable way in the home territory for several weeks. Even in the fall, it seems that some of these family groups may still be intact. They migrate southward for the winter as they are insectivorous in feeding habits, but they supplement their diet with wild berries. 18cm. (7")

American Redstart, *Setophaga ruticilla.* (female) In summer, this redstart ranges over the greater part of North America, north of Mexico, wherever there are forests. It builds its nests in almost any kind of habitat, but it shows a preference for deciduous cover and damp situations. It may return annually to the same spot as it has a strong homing instinct. 13cm. (5")

Blackburnian Warbler, *Dendroica fusca.* (male) During the summer, the Blackburnian Warbler is found frequently in the tall conifers where it nests. At other times, it may be observed in deciduous trees as well as coniferous. It is an eastern species, Saskatchewan forming the western limit of its range. Apparently it was named for a European naturalist by the name of *Blackburn.* 13 cm. (5")

American Tree Sparrow, *Spizella arborea.* "I really do like you; could we be pals again?" 16 cm. (6.5")

furnish the date, location, and manner in which the bird was obtained. Then, add your name and address. The banding office will furnish information on the history of the bird. If the bird is alive, it is understood that you will release it and so inform the banding office. Send your correspondance to the appropriate office as listed below: Bird Banding Laboratory, Office of Migratory Bird Management, Laurel, Maryland 20708. Canadian Wildlife Service, 2721 Highway 31, Ottawa, Ontario, K1A 0E3, Canada.

Some of the most interesting facts discovered to date are where birds travel seasonally, whether they stick to a certain flyway, how long it takes them to make the journey, whether they have homing ability, and how long they live. Some birds can find their "homes" both in summer and in winter. I was impressed when one of the first birds I banded in winter, an American Tree Sparrow, found its way back again to the same farm field where it was banded one year previously. In this way, as might be guessed, more band returns may be handled by banders than by the general public. Bird-banding is not new. There are records in early history of scientists marking birds in order to learn of their travels.

As indicated above, bird-banding is kept under rather rigid control. To obtain a permit, the applicant must have a definite research program with certain goals in mind and a plan to publish or otherwise make available the facts leaned. Under most permit arrangements, the bander must be able to recognize accurately the majority of the birds found in his region, for to place a band on a misnamed bird would defeat the purpose. (Some birds look differently at close range than in their natural habitat.) He must be recommended by competent authorities. In this respect, beginners often work for a while as sub-permittees under the supervision of seasoned banders. Bird-banding organizations hold conventions which, among other things, enable banders to become acquainted with one another.

The kinds of traps used may be controlled by the permit. Special traps, often needed, are not sold to the public but only to those who can produce an active permit number. As a rule, all birds must be banded and released within a short time, so the traps in operation must be continually watched. If they were neglected, considerable loss of birdlife would result. Careful and rather lengthy reports must be maintained and sent in regularly. All in all, banding is a pretty big undertaking.

Much important work is conducted today by professional workers, especially in the management field. I shall have more to say about this in my chapter on bird research.

Bird Rehabilitation

Most active birders, it seems, are persuaded at one time or another in their careers to attempt to rehabilitate a wounded bird or to care for an orphan. In order to do this legally, permits are needed as the work usually involves possession of protected species. Incidentally when farmers or other workers find a nest of eggs for which the parent birds were accidentally killed by machinery, they often may obtain a permit to hatch them. Such permits, though, have practical application primarily when the birds in question are precocial and can run about shortly after hatching. Because of the specialized nature of the work, rehabilitation permits are restricted largely to specialists.

To rehabilitate a bird, whether it is ill or crippled, is a difficult task. To attempt to raise an orphan (if it really is an orphan) is often a disappointing experience, for to provide the variety of food needed is usually inconven-

Eastern Meadowlark, *Sturnella magna.* Of all the birds found on our eastern farms, this meadowlark is probably one of the best known. I can remember watching them many years ago on my uncle's farm, as they flushed from the ground to land on the fence posts. They sputtered as they flew. They are not restricted to the open habitat, though; in the Gulf States, for example, many can be found in open groves of pine trees. 25 cm. (10")

Bell's Vireo, *Vireo bellii.* Most Bell's Vireo's that I have seen have been associated with plum thickets, but they are not restricted to them. Fences of multiflora rose, for example, are a great help to them in the Midwest. They construct their nests in such habitat, at almost any height above the ground. Audubon named the species for his friend, J.G. Bell. 13 cm. (5")

American Tree Sparrow, *Spizella arborea.* The nesting range of this sparrow extends from Labrador to Alaska and northern British Columbia, and takes in most of the taiga and much of the tundra. Imagine my delight, therefore, when a Tree Sparrow which I had banded in a farm field one year, came back to the same field the following year, this field being its winter quarters (southern Wisconsin). 16cm. (6.5")

Magnolia Warbler, *Dendroica magnolia.* (male) There is no special significance attached to the name Magnolia. Alexander Wilson so named the species when he encountered his first specimen in a magnolia tree in Mississippi. The bird shows a preference for coniferous forests when nesting, but it may be found in deciduous growth during migration. 13cm. (5")

ient. Often used for this purpose are yokes of hard-boiled eggs, meal worms, crickets, moths, canned pet food, mashed berries or nut meats, and the like. Soft foods must be fed to young birds, but more solid or hard foods can be fed to adult birds.

When so-called orphans are brought in it may be possible to locate the parent birds or the nest. In such cases, the young birds are better off returned to the care of their parents.

If members of the heron family are to be rehabilitated, care should be exercised lest they go for one's eyes. They can strike with lightning speed.

Racing Pigeons

Rock Doves, our well-known "pigeons," have been used to carry messages throughout history. Some historians believe that the practice began in the Middle East. Today, we find many devotees in western Europe and in North America. Such birds have often been used in wartime by army officers, large numbers being employed occasionally to deliver strategic information. The darker birds are preferred for this purpose as they are the least likely to be noticed by the enemy. (More recently, a new use has been found for them. They deliver prescription medicine quickly.)

Rock Doves go by many names. Because they carry messages, they may be called "carriers." Since they return home quickly and accurately, they are called "homing pigeons." As many are seen about farm buildings, they are called "barn pigeons." The reason why they are called "racing pigeons" is a little more roundabout. After the birds have been put through certain prescribed routines, they are raced to see how fast they can perform.

Racing pigeons are often found by the public and

reported to governmental agencies. On the bird's legs may be found two bands. A rubber band, bearing numbers, indicates that the bird is in a race. A metal band, bearing a legend, serves to identify the owner.

Sometimes it is difficult to get stray birds to leave one's premises. The thing to do in this case is to give the bird (usually there is only one) a drink of cool water, a small amount of grain such as rice, wheat, oats, or corn (but not bread), and house it overnight in a box which will admit air. In the early morning, give it another drink of water, but no food. Then release it. If it persists in staying, take it out into the wilderness and release it. It should eventually get back to its home.

Everyone should bear in mind that racing pigeons are valuable and protected by law in most regions. Many of them are pedigreed. Most races for pigeons are run during the spring and fall seasons. Rock Doves are remarkable for their speed and endurance. Many can fly all day without stopping. Some are able to do 805 kilometers (500 miles) in a day. When flying over water, they have a tendency to speed up. A few do not make it back home, but the majority succeed remarkably well.

Though the hobby of raising pigeons is somewhat specialized it is within the reach of almost anyone who is interested. A loft can be built in the back yard. Feeding is simple, as the birds need only two meals per day. Separate nest boxes are needed for each pair. When birds return to the loft, a trap door admits them, but also prevents them from escaping. Their quarters must be kept clean, rainproof, and relatively free from drafts, but this is not difficult to arrange. All pigeons need a generous supply of clean, cool water to drink. Current information on their care and training can be obtained from the various racing pigeon associations. The addresses of the latter change periodically, but the

Rock Dove, *Columba livia.* Rock Doves, as indicated in the name, nest and live often in the vicinity of rock cliffs (in our western states, there are many such instances), but the majority find living in the vicinity of man to be more compatible. Thus we find them nesting in buildings and under bridges or similar structures. 33 cm. (13″)

Rock Dove, *Columba livia.* Illustrated here is a homing pigeon. Today such birds may be found in almost any color combination as they readily interbreed. Some operators, however, still use the original type with the white rump. We call this form the Rock Dove. When these birds were first used to carry messages is unknown, but there are records in ancient history. 33 cm. (13″)

Fulvous Whistling-Duck, *Dendrocygna bicolor.* For many years, this species was known as one of our tree ducks, but it rarely perches in trees, so the new name is more appropriate. (Fulvous refers to the dominant color of the plumage.) In common with the other *whistling* species, it stands tall, having relatively long legs and neck. (I obtained my photograph in Florida.) 48cm. (19")

Anhinga, *Anhinga anhinga.* The female shown here, differs from the male, mainly in that her head, neck, and upper breast area is buffy-brown. She is taking a rest after feeding in the nearby fresh-water habitat. The sharply-pointed bill of the species is serrated at the tip, thus enabling the birds to hold on to their prey. 89cm. (35")

larger libraries often keep up-to-date on these matters, and many governmental agencies concerned with birds keep in touch.

Rock Doves can breed throughout the year; in fact, some may lay a new set of eggs before the young of the previous set have flown. It takes about four weeks for a chick to attain full size and one additional week for it to fly. Both parents incubate the two eggs and care for the young. Although the birds can produce many broods annually, most operators limit their birds to three or four broods per year in order to conserve their strength. Rock Doves are comparatively long-lived.

Collecting Birds

Early day ornithologists collected birds, their nests, and eggs rather freely. There was need to identify the various species, to establish their ranges, and to determine their food habits. Many early bird painters collected their subjects whenever they were ready to start a painting.

Today collecting permits are more restrictive. The need for collecting is not as great as it once was. Sometimes permits to temporarily hold a live bird for certain studies will suffice. Museum personnel generally keep collecting permits on hand for obvious reasons, and research specialists often need them. Some professional ornithologists need a permit occasionally.

Essentially, a collector's permit allows the individual to collect and possess specimens at any time of the year. Guns or other legal means can be used to obtain the specimens, but large numbers of good specimens can be picked up at television towers, airport ceilometers, tall buildings, and the like. When a private collector secures specimens, he usually skins them himself and may mount them as well, but all specimens must eventually end up in a public museum. In other words, there is no private ownership involved, and the meat is not legal as food.

Today, teachers and other individuals innocently collect old nests for class use or other commendable reasons. Unfortunately, this cannot be done without a collector's permit. The point is, there is no way to prove that the nests were not taken while they were in active use. Without this legal restriction anyone could collect active nests and eggs at will.

Along with the permit goes a great responsibility on the part of the collector. Good public relations must be maintained. Where and when to shoot often becomes a sensitive question. Needless trips to distant points by conservation wardens sometimes are caused by thoughtless collectors.

Professional Taxidermy

The preservation of valuable wildlife specimens, including birds, is now a flourishing business. Shops have sprung up almost everywhere. Professional taxidermists who do this work need permits to prepare protected species, and the customers, of course, need permits to possess them. Professional taxidermists are limited to game legally taken during open seasons.

Laws Protecting Birds

In the foregoing sections, I have mentioned laws that are likely to apply under certain circumstances. The reason for doing this is to acquaint our newcomers with some of the problems. A few of the laws referred to will not apply uniformly throughout the land, and some will change in various ways from year to year. Thus, to obtain current information, it is necessary for those who are interested to check with their local authorities.

Tennessee Warbler, *Vermivora peregrina.* (male) The song of this warbler is loud and piercing. As a friend of mine put it, while taking a May Day Count, "You don't have to get out of the car to hear that!" The nesting range is widespread in Canada, but it seems that the majority of the birds migrate to the east of the Rocky Mountains. Wilson named the species for the state where it was first discovered. 13 cm. (5")

Red-eyed Vireo, *Vireo olivaceus.* Although we have many kinds of vireos, it seems that this species is the best-known, and the one with which many others are compared. To be sure, it gives the listener ample opportunity to become acquainted, for it sings from dawn to dusk throughout the entire nesting season. 15 cm. (6")

Tufted Titmouse, *Parus bicolor.* When I lived in Virginia, I noticed that many people called these birds *see-dads.* This name was imitative of the sound heard incessantly when family groups traveled together. Such groups were conspicuous in rural areas wherever there were groves of trees. Of course, the adults had other calls, the most common being the *peto* call, often repeated. 15 cm. (6″)

American Robin, *Turdus migratorius.* (male) When I lived in North Carolina, I enjoyed the large wintering flocks of robins that gathered in the canebreaks, for, on days when the temperature was higher than usual, some of the birds would sing snatches of their spring song. Now that I have moved farther north, I look forward to the return of the migrants. 25 cm. (10″)

Chapter 2

NATURE'S CHECKS & BALANCES

A few years ago, a pair of American Crows decided to nest in my back yard. I am not especially fond of crows, but I was pleased to see them because I wanted to make some studies of their nesting habits. The crow had no sooner laid its eggs when a squirrel came along and devoured them. Well, I lost my chance to study the crows, but I was forcibly reminded that Nature has her own controls.

In the plant kingdom, also, there are natural controls. A plant that has grown tall as the result of copious rains may succumb easily to drought. When vegetation grows up thickly, lightning may strike, burn a portion of it, and thus thin it out. It is not neccessary to expand on how insects can damage plants.

Our birds participate in the control of about everything in the animal kingdom and in control of certain plants. In like manner, about everything in the animal kingdom participates in the control of our birds. Certain plants exercise control over birds too, but this is generally indirect. To illustrate, a certain niche in the habitat will support a bird well enough for it to succeed, but poorly enough to restrict its numbers. Or, plant succession may, in due time, render the habitat unsuitable for a given species. In addition to controls from without, some birds have population controls that are "built in." In this way Nature checks the growth and expansion of all her elements and keeps them in balance. The system works well when Nature is left to her own devices but, unfortunately, rather poorly when man interferes.

The Harmony Upset

I do not believe that man has intentionally upset the balance of Nature. Much damage has been done by him through ignorance or for economic reasons. Good habitat has been destroyed by the development of industry, farming, and recreation; many primitive areas have been polluted with chemicals. Birds have died in great numbers because of poisons that have been spread far and wide. Historically, man has reduced the populations of certain species of birds by unregulated hunting. He has stocked birds foreign to our country, only to find that they have become a nuisance rather than a help. Certain species of birds have become too plentiful as a result of man's management of the environment.

Unfortunately, planting large acreages of one crop upsets the balance of Nature. Insects, destructive to this crop, multiply beyond all reason under such circumstances. Birds and the other natural checks on insects cannot keep up with them. A similar situation prevails in cities when trees are set out, all of the same species. Any insect or disease that comes along is likely to take all of them. To further complicate the picture, insects foreign to our country have been imported, either intentionally or by accident. Many of these, being out of place, are more destructive than native species.

There was a period in American history when man, wishing to defend the existence of nongame birds, explained that they ate insects destructive to man's interests. This was done on the basis of food habit studies conducted by ornithologists and other scientists of the day. Along with this, came leaders in the field who stressed the aesthetic side of birds, and still others spoke of their emotional value. While intentions were good, these people did not understand the basic reason

Ruby-throated Humming-bird, *Archilochus colubris.* (male) Hummingbirds regularly visit our flower gardens, and more birds are probably seen here than elsewhere, but they may be looked for in our marshes when flowers are in bloom (especially in the fall), and in open woodlands. In the latter habitat, they may visit the *wells* of sapsuckers in order to obtain insects as well as some of the sap. 9 cm. (3.5")

Barn Swallow, *Hirundo rustica.* This is the swallow with the deeply forked tail. It flies low where everyone can see it, is elegant in appearance, and nests throughout much of the North American continent. The fact that it builds its nest in barns also is a plus, for it helps to rid the premises of objectionable insects. 18 cm. (7")

Common Yellowthroat, *Geothlypis trichas.* (female) We see yellow-throats often in wet habitat such as brushy swamps, the edges of marshes, and along streams, but they can be found in the uplands. They are inquisitive in nature and remind us of wrens as they move about. The females (usually) build their nests often on the ground with only a few tufts of grass or weeds to furnish cover. 13cm. (5")

Palm Warbler, *Dendroica palmarum.* I took this photograph in September, but I cannot tell the exact age of the bird. It is the western form. Palm Warblers may be observed in the northern parts of their range as late as November, as they can eat wild berries if their insect food fails. It seems that someone in the winter range named the species. 13cm. (5")

why birds are a part of the harmony of Nature. Instead they thought of ways in which birds could *serve* man. There were also people who contended that the only good "predator" was a *dead* "predator."

The Awakening

Fortunately, there has been an awakening. Leaders in the field have succeeded in focusing our attention upon the plight in which we find ourselves. It is now generally agreed that we need to "clean up" our entire environment. This causes us to wonder why action has been so slow in coming. Knowledge on many facets of the subject has been available for years.

While reading Gilbert White's *The Natural History of Selborne* one day, I noticed that in the eighteenth century it was known that worms helped to aerate the soil. In the early part of the twentieth century, if not before, it was known that lady beetles were effective in checking populations of plant lice.

American Indians were aware of the subject. In 1855, Chief Sealth of the Duwanish wrote: *"Every* part of the earth is sacred to my people." And in making an appraisal of the white man, he sadly observed, "The earth is not his brother, but his enemy."[1]

We do not like to admit it, but the last phrase of this quotation is the *key* to most of our outdoor problems. Sometimes we think that interference on our part in the harmony of Nature affects only the wild things. This is not true. When we upset the balance of Nature, we upset our own balance! We do not always recognize the symptoms, for they come only a few at a time.

As Confucius said, "Men do not stumble over

---

[1] From a letter written and sent to President Franklin Pierce, in 1855, by Chief Sealth of the Duwanish Tribe. Recorded by the Kentucky Department of Fish and Wildlife Resources.

mountains, but over molehills." Or, as Albert Schweitzer observed, "Man has lost the capacity to foresee and to forestall. He will end up by destroying the earth." But, when man sees impending danger to himself, he does take action.

The Restoration

We are now in the process of restoring the "balance of Nature." Whether we will be entirely successful remains to be seen. First of all, to be fair about it, we have not ruined *everything* in Nature. Surveys show that many species of birds, for example, are doing just as well today as they were a century ago. Some species are actually doing better. The same can be said for certain mammals and the other forms. Thus as a first priority, we are trying to maintain the *status quo.*

Secondly, as far as the birds are concerned, we are making an all-out effort to replenish those species that are becoming rare.

Thirdly, we are studying the pristine areas that remain in order to learn how to duplicate them in the future.

While speed is paramount in these matters, we know that there will be delays in our restoration program. Only recently, a friend of mine quipped, "Everybody can see that the world needs changing, but everybody wants to start with that part farthest removed from himself." Another delay may come in some of our restoration projects because of man's tendency to "hurry up." If we skip some of the steps which Nature requires, we may fail to reach our goal. Nature takes her time, so for man to duplicate something quickly may be impossible.

We dare not confuse the above "hurry up" with the urgency to get started. Only recently, I heard of a House

Connecticut Warbler, *Oporornis agilis.* (female) The nesting range of this warbler extends in a rather narrow band from Quebec to British Columbia, but the bird is practically unknown in the western half of the United States and in Mexico. Its winter range is in northern South America, so it seems that the majority of the birds migrate by way of Florida. 14 cm. (5.5″)

Downy Woodpecker, *Picoides pubescens.* (male) The Downy Woodpecker has won for itself the reputation of being a sociable creature, for it often keeps company with such species as chickadees, nuthatches, and titmice, especially in winter. Thus we find it in the woodland edges and suburbs of cities. In farming country, it forages in the corn fields, extracting insects from the corn stalks and weed stalks that are found there. 16 cm. (6.5″)

Eastern Kingbird, *Tyrannus tyrannus.* Eastern Kingbirds are noisy, and in keeping with their name, quite dominant within their nesting territories. They have the courage to go after their potential enemies long before they come near, and it does not seem to matter how large they are. They are birds of the open, or semiopen country, and if water is present, they may nest in its vicinity. 20cm. (8")

Common Grackle, *Quiscalus quiscula.* (male) The iridescent plumage of the male, though appearing to be black from a distance, varies in color geographically. Purple is prominent in parts of the East, and bronze is dominent in the remainder of the range, particularly in the Midwest. The female is duller in color and smaller than the male. My photograph of the male was taken in the Midwest. 33cm. (13")

Sparrow that, while constructing its nest in the eaves of a building, brought in a piece of material which it found at a burning grounds. This was still smouldering so a fire was started. Perhaps the bird was trying to tell us something. After all, haven't we been burning up good bird habitat for years!

Economic Problems

Economic problems will cause serious delays in our restoration programs. Also, we expect that there will be some "give and take." In order to stimulate thinking along these lines, I shall include below some examples of subjects that often come up for discussion. (This is not to say that I have answers to all the problems involved. I do not.)

Birds and Insects

That birds feed on insects, spiders, worms, and the like, is well known. Many other creatures also feed on them. As this phenomenon is a part of the ecological picture, we shall expect that birds, among other creatures, will eat insects without regard for man's economic interests. Further, we shall not expect them to sharply control any of the insects. From man's viewpoint, many of our native insects and some of the exotic species are beneficial. Some of our native insects and many of our importations are destructive to man's interests. When birds feed on insects that are injurious, we generally say that they render man a service.

Man has tried many ways in which to control or eliminate destructive insects. Many of his methods have backfired, but it now appears that he is on the right track. He is pitting one insect against another.

Insects are needed by man to cross-pollinate such things as medicinal plants, hybrid seeds, hay, melons, cabbage and related vegetables, onions, carrots and related roots, sunflowers, spices, and various ornamentals. Their service in cross-pollinating plants far outweighs any damage they do. They eat only a portion of the crops which they themselves help to provide. How could we economically cross-pollinate all the plants without the help of insects?

Insects serve man in unexpected ways. Today, for example, scientists can predict earthquakes by the actions of certain insects. As scavengers, insects are unexcelled. They clean up the environment.

Many wild things need insects in their diets. Included in the list are other insects, bacteria, viruses, fungi, protozoans, nemotodes, bats, armadillos, bears, badgers, certain squirrels, moles, shrews, mice, toads, frogs, lizards, snakes, fish, and of course, birds. Those birds that commonly feed on vegetable matter often feed insects to their nestlings.

Birds and Plants

Plants, as everyone knows, furnish habitat and food for birds. What is not so well known is how birds can help plants. Hummingbirds and certain other species help to cross pollinate plants. The seed-eaters help to develop habitat when they regurgitate or pass seeds that are still in viable conditon. Birds are helpful to plants, also, when they remove certain insects from their leaves and branches.

Some Thoughts On Predation

Predation occurs throughout the wild kingdom and is necessary to continue the balance in Nature. When studying ecology, we realize this clearly. Thus I assume that no one will take a prejudicial view of those creatures that are designated as "predators." Conversely,

Cedar Waxwing, *Bombycilla cedrorum.* The expression, "here today and gone tomorrow," has application with waxwings, for, instead of gathering their food a little here and a little there as many birds do, they are prone to remain in one spot until all food supplies are exhausted. As they come in large flocks, the supplies dwindle rapidly, thus causing the birds to wander widely, sometimes well beyond their usual ranges. 18cm. (7")

American Robin, *Turdus migratorius.* (female) Robins will eat almost anything that is edible. It is well-known that they feed on worms, insects, and small fruits; what is not so well-known is that they will also eat small snakes and small shrews. Hairy caterpillars are often shunned by birds in general, but the robin has a way of scraping off the objectionable hairs. 25cm. (10")

Northern Flicker, *Colaptes auratus.* (male) Flickers are woodpeckers, but they differ basically from most other members of their family in the way they feed. They spend much of their time on the ground where they find ants to eat. Three forms, known respectively as Yellow-shafted, Red-shafted, and Gilded, are now combined under the above species name. The form in my photograph is the Yellow-shafted. 33cm. (13")

Turkey Vulture, *Cathartes aura.* Turkey Vultures are primarily flesh-eaters, but they are not equipped to capture anything that is very lively. Thus we find them scouring the countryside in search of carcasses. If they sight one, which they can do from afar, several vultures usually will gather to particpate in the meal. (In the Tropics, Turkey Vultures are known to eat some plant foods such as overripe fruits.) 76cm. (30") **115**

I take it for granted that no one will try to obtain preferential treatment for a branch of the wild kingdom that happens to be his favorite (endangered species excepted). All normal elements are on a par in Nature.

Hawks, owls, gulls, and other birds that kill birds and other creatures are commonly called "predators." The view sometimes taken is that these so-called predators do not have many natural checks, so must be controlled by man. This is unfortunate, for they actually do have their share of natural checks, some of which are "built in."

Most of the so-called predators lay small sets of eggs, and when these hatch, one of the larger nestlings may turn on one of the smaller ones. In some cases, adults also may feed on nestlings, but not their own as a rule. In those years when food is in short supply, some hawks or owls may not lay any eggs at all. Parasites and diseases cause many of them to die prematurely. The falcons sometimes kill owls for food, and jays often kill the smaller species of owls, not for food necessarily, but in order to get rid of a potential nuisance. The larger owls prey upon the falcons. Golden Eagles are known to kill and eat hawks and falcons of various species. As a general rule, hawks and owls avoid nesting near one another, so this, in itself, becomes a curb on their numbers. By nesting early, and because of its great size, the Great Horned Owl discourages many of the hawks from nesting nearby. Raccoons devour the eggs of hawks and owls. When poisonous snakes are sought as food, they often turn on their attackers with success.

Gulls, sometimes called "predators," nest on the ground, so they are restricted to areas such as islands where ground enemies are virtually absent. As suitable islands are scarce, their numbers are automatically controlled. If they do find a suitable place to nest, they still have to face their avian "predators."

Sometimes unusual conditions invite "predators" to visit a given place more often than usual. When a problem of this kind arises, permits to control the offenders can usually be obtained. Methods of control vary. If a rare species is involved, it may be live-trapped and moved to a distant point.

In Europe, as well as in America, it has been found that hawks usually do not look for food near their own nests. In fact, many species of small birds (and sometimes large birds) take advantage of the protection afforded to them by the presence of hawks. Often small birds have been found nesting in the outer pockets of active hawk nests. Since the hawk's food is gleaned from far and wide, no particular prey population has to bear the brunt. (Aristotle wrote of this habit among certain eagles, many centuries ago.) Their food items include mammals, reptiles, amphibians, birds, insects, and many other things, thus lightening the blow still more. Only those food species that are most common make up the bulk of the diet of any "predator." The fact that these common species maintain their numbers, demonstrates that they can withstand the pressure.

When "predators" capture the diseased and weak, they perform a service to the species involved by keeping it strong. When fish become overpopulated, they do not grow to full size but remain stunted. Thus if fish-eating birds or other predators reduce their numbers, they render a service to the fish and to the fisherman. People who eliminate predatory birds or mammals that feed on upland game birds, for example, also may be eliminating the natural controls of rodents which, in turn, devour the food supplies of the game birds in question.

Predation in any form may be useful to a prey

Barred Owl, *Strix varia.* Because of its loud hooting and relatively large numbers, this species is probably our best-known owl. In my opinion, it is responsible for the term, *hoot-owl,* which also is applied often to certain other species. It can be seen abroad quite regularly during the day, and its calls can be heard at almost any hour. 53 cm. (21")

Common Barn-Owl, *Tyto alba.* Barn-Owls are ghostlike in appearance, and in harmony with this, they are reluctant to be seen. Usually they go abroad only during the hours of darkness, unless they find it desirable to attend to their young at other times. They are able to call loudly, but seldom do; only an occasional *snore,* or a clicking sound of the bill, is normally heard. 43 cm. (17")

Swainson's Hawk, *Buteo swainsoni.* Swainson's Hawk is a bird of the open spaces, including the deserts. Frequently, it may be seen resting on fence posts and other low perches along the roadsides. When in flight, its wings appear to be more ample than those of the Redtail, and when sailing, the bird holds its wings more in Turkey Vulture-fashion (v-shape). 53 cm. (21")

Red-tailed Hawk, *Buteo jamaicensis.* This hawk may be observed along the edges of woodlands where it commonly builds its nest, or in trees of the more open country where it either takes life easy or watches for its prey. Its distinctive cry, a piercing *kre-ee-ee* (uttered often while in flight), brings the bird to our attention. 56 cm. (22")

species when it interrupts the nesting cycle. If all birds laid their eggs at the same time, for example, a weather catastrophe could wipe out all production for the year. By forcing the birds to stretch out their nesting season (which predation may do), at least a certain contingent of the population will have a chance to succeed.

Further Economic Considerations

Most species of our native birds are useful to man or at least neutral in the economic sense. They destory unwanted insects, rodents, and weed seeds, and serve as scavengers. Many furnish food and sport for sportsmen. Some furnish essential food and products of commerce. All furnish recreation and enjoyment to millions of people who travel long distances in order to observe them. The money spent in America for the enjoyment of birds, directly or indirectly, runs into millions of dollars annually.

Some birds have served in special ways too. Only recently, the danger of pesticides and other forms of pollution to man was "brought home" to us through experiments with the raptors (hawks and owls). The Rock Dove has saved the lives of many soldiers by carrying messages during wartime.

Some areas in which birds commonly do damage to man are the following: grain fields, fruit orchards, berry patches, truck gardens, airports, city suburbs (blackbird roosts), and cities (pigeon and starling nuisance). Occasionally, disease is involved which affects either man himself or his farm stock. Most of these diseases are associated with birds which have been imported by man. Provision has been made by many governmental agencies to reimburse the private landowner for damage caused by certain species of birds which otherwise are desirable.

As birds are helpful to some people and a

hinderance to others, we do not expect perfect agreement on these matters. The word "tolerance" comes to mind. In a democracy, we tolerate what the majority wants.

The Upshot

"Birders can go to the zoo to see birds if the wild ones disappear," quipped a bystander, after listening to parts of a convention on environmental matters. More people take a view of Nature in this way than we would care to admit. As one authority put it many years ago, "Man is too far removed (now in cities) to know the workings of Nature."

What can we do about it?

Obviously, we need to continue working with our children. They are not prejudiced by nature against any of Nature's wildlings. School forests, Nature trails, and the like are excellent places in which to explain the interrelationships of the various forms of life and how they need one another. Here, the instructor can demonstrate how the bluebird depends upon the woodpecker to construct a home for it, how the beaver helps the ducks by impounding water, or how the robin depends upon the tree in which it nests to leaf out eventually and hide its nest.

Surely, as the young people understand how *all* links in the chain are needed, they will do all in their power to prevent extinction of even one species. We do not yet know all the uses a certain animal or plant might have. How many plants have we exterminated, for example, that could have been used for medicinal purposes?

Care should be exercised to make sure that our children get an accurate report. Unfortunately, much of what they hear today is calculated to make heroes out of

Golden Eagle, *Aquila chrysaetos.* Throughout the years, ornithologists have given the Golden Eagle a high rating among our birds of prey. Certainly it is strong and daring—more so than the Bald Eagle, for example—and one that has maintained a representative population in spite of persecution. It often nests in cliffs. 89 cm. (35")

Harris' Hawk, *Parabuteo unicinctus.* When perched in a tree at a distance, this species appears to be almost wholly dark. At close range, though, the rusty shoulders and thighs can be seen. The bird may be looked for in either partly wooded or desert habitat. It has been observed to raise more than one brood, annually, and this is unusual among hawks. 51 cm. (20")

Black-billed Cuckoo, *Coccyzus erythropthalmus.* The name *cuckoo* has its origin in the Old World. It refers to the bird's call. In America, the connection is not so apparent. Neither do our cuckoos parasitize the nests of other birds as a regular procedure, although they may do so occasionally. Both parents incubate the eggs and care for the young as a general rule. 30 cm. (12″)

Ringed Turtle-Dove, *Streptopelia risoria.* This species is not native to North America, but it has become established in such cities as Los Angeles and Tampa, as a result of releases. Reports of it may be expected in new places at any time. I recently saw one flying about in the trees on the south side of Carlsbad, New Mexico. 30 cm. (12″)

some animals and villains out of others. It is necessary to undo this in our educational programs, for in Nature, there are no "saints" or "sinners." When a bird eats the eggs of another bird, it does not feel any differently about it than it does when it eats an insect. It is simply following its role in Nature.

Education in environmental matters of any kind is useful to everyone, regardless of age, for disputes on such matters are frequently taken to court. It is the informed individual who is in the best position to win.

Chapter 3

INTERESTING ASPECTS
OF THE WAYS OF BIRDS

"The lower animals have not the high advantages which we have, but they have some which we lack."
—Montesquieu

Many years ago, a wren house which I had put up in our garden was raided by a cat. Apparently the mother wren and one or two nestlings were seized. Knowing that the father had been assisting with the care of the young, I assumed that the remaining young would be provided for. On the next night, however, the cat (not mine) returned and captured these also. (We had tomato vines tied to the pole, so I had not attached an inverted metal cone to prevent the cat from climbing to the house.) The thing that amazed me and the point of my story is that, on the very next day, the father began anew to sing vigorously and incessantly. I was convinced from this experience that birds do not necessarily reason in the same way people do. In the stories that follow, this quirk will surface again and again.

The Nesting Cycle

The majority of North American birds begin their nesting activities in the spring. It is thought that these activities are correlated with the climate and weather in such a way as to favor the offspring. Not all species are "geared" to the same calendar, though; some starting in midwinter, some during the summer, and some at almost any time. I shall start my discussion with matters pertaining to the nesting territory, as it is here that the

American Woodcock, *Scolopax minor.* The nest site of the woodcock, shown here, was situated in a small opening in the forest, and near the forest edge. This is a typical location for the species. The eggs are laid at an early date as indicated by the presence of bloodroot blossoms. 28cm. (11″)

Black-and-white Warbler, *Mniotilta varia.* (female) When feeding, this warbler creeps high into the trees, but when it is ready to build its nest, it looks for a site on or near the ground. Such nests are not easily seen, though, for the bird builds a canopy of leaves or other debris over them. The species is widespread in North America during the nesting season, but its numbers thin out west of the Rocky Mountains. 13cm. (5″)

Bonaparte's Gull, *Larus philadelphia.* This species is slightly smaller than the better-known Laughing Gull. Its nesting range lies chiefly in Canada, and contrary to what we would expect, in the forested regions. The birds nest in trees, usually conifers, at moderate heights above the ground. (The bird shown here is in immature plumage; I photographed it in April.) 35 cm. (14")

Indigo Bunting, *Passerina cyanea.* (female) Buntings nest in mixed habitat such as cut-over forest land, roadside shrubbery, and waste-land. Usually there is a tall tree in the complex to accomodate the male when he sings. The female, in my experience, does not often show herself. The nesting range lies mainly to the east of the Rocky Mountains. 14 cm. (5.5")

more significant activities take place. However, I should mention at the start that not all species use their nesting territories to the same degree or in the same way. Among waterfowl, for example, some species arrive upon their nesting grounds already paired.

Requirements Of The Territory

During the past summer, a pair of American Robins built a nest in my front yard. The material for the nest was gathered within 61 meters (200 ft.) of the nest, and as far as I could tell, the food for the nestlings was collected mostly within 46 meters (150 ft.). It seems that all their requirements were met within about the same confines. (This is not to say that all robins will be restricted to such a small nesting territory. Many are not.)

Recently, I photographed some Cattle Egrets in a cow pasture. This was their feeding territory. Their nesting territory, I found out later, was in a marsh where certain other egrets and herons were nesting. Thus their total requirements were not met in the same place. They needed at least two kinds of habitat.

While in Texas some years ago, I watched a Greater Prairie-Chicken dance on what we call a "booming ground." (The noise the cocks make is thought to be a booming sound.) This booming ground was separate from the nesting and feeding areas, so this species requires a special place for courtship.

There are many other variations. In general, though, a nesting territory is a place where a pair of birds can find suitable facilities for raising their young. The boundaries would include whatever the birds try to defend. (Incidentally, not all species defend territories.)

Picking The Territory

Banding records show that many species return to the same nesting territories year after year. This may apply both to the adults and to the young. Because certain species have a proclivity to return to their former haunts, wide gaps may exist in their breeding ranges. There may be a northern and a southern population, for example, in a given species, and for these two populations the egg-laying dates may differ considerably.

Not all species have the homing instinct, but when birds, either adult or immature, migrate to their breeding ranges, they usually are able to recognize the niche of their species. Some are so reliable in this way that an ornithologist, upon developing a piece of new habitat, can predict what will occupy it.

There is more to the art of selecting a nesting territory than meets the eye. If, for example, a bird builds its nest in a bare tree or shrub, how does it know that the foliage needed to shelter the young, will develop later? Conversely, if a tree by its nature sheds its leaves in late spring, how do the birds that nest early know that they should avoid it?

Defending The Territory

One day while searching for wildflowers and birds in southern Saskatchewan, my party noticed a female Wilson's Phalarope flying in wide circles over our heads and calling nervously. We had entered its nesting territory so the bird was upset. Our intrusion led to a further development. In its efforts to drive us out, the phalarope had gotten into the nesting territory of an Eastern Kingbird. The latter, in turn, became very belligerent and chased the phalarope away.

Recently, someone in my office called my attention to an American Crow running along a window sill and

Yellow-bellied Flycatcher, *Empidonax flaviventris.* This species is unique among our flycatchers in that it nests regularly on the ground. In our northern bogs where many of these birds spend the summer, the nests may be sunk to the rim in mossy or spongy soil. The yellowish throat is a help in identification if the yellowish belly cannot be seen. 14 cm. (5.5")

Yellow-rumped Warbler, *Dendroica coronata.* (female) This warbler prefers to nest in conifers. Usually the nest is built on a horizontal limb, and this can be at almost any height above the ground. The female, shown here, is the *Myrtle* form of the named species. Its range is widespread in North America, but that of the *Audubon* form is limited to the West. 14 cm. (5.5")

Solitary Sandpiper, *Tringa solitaria.* Differing from many of its relatives, the Solitary Sandpiper commonly shuns the wide-open marshes in order to enjoy the solitude of a wooded stream or pond. Incredible as it seems, the bird uses deserted nests of such land birds as blackbirds and robins. The nests selected can be situated at almost any height in a tree. 20 cm. (8″)

Cliff Swallow, *Hirundo pyrrhonota.* Originally these swallows nested on the sides of cliffs and in caves. Today, they still nest as they once did, especially in our wilderness habitats, but they also make use of such structures as barns and bridges. The nest-colony (active) shown here was located in northern New Mexico. 14 cm. (5.5″)

continually pecking at the window glass. It could see its image in the window and thought that another crow was competing for its territory.

Thus, birds may drive away competitors of either their own kind or of another species. Defense of the territory is taken seriously, and in some species, blood may flow. The latter is rare, however, as the "intruder" usually backs down.

Not all territorial defense is conducted in the same way. Many ornithologists are convinced that vigorous singing on the part of the male may, in itself, serve to stave off competitors. Those birds that are able to increase their size by ruffing out their feathers, no doubt, have a distinct advantage. Among colonial species, many birds may be involved simultaneously in territorial defense.

Territorial defense is not limited to the nesting season in all species. Some may defend territories at any time. I think of the Northern Mockingbird in this connection.

Does Territorial Defense Do Anything For The Species As A Whole?

The strongest males secure the best territories as a rule, and because of their dominance, regularly acquire mates. The theory implies that the males to be squeezed out are the younger, inexperienced, or weaker individuals. Some of these may enter the picture later in the nesting season though, if a dominant male is killed. Territorial defense serves to expand the breeding range of the species, and this is a help for obvious reasons. Any system that serves to scatter the species somewhat helps to remove the threat of disease and other disasters. If it serves to repel certain competitive species, territorial defense becomes an equalizing force in the balance of Nature.

Territorial defense also has certain disadvantages to the species as a whole. This is axiomatic in Nature. Otherwise there would be no checks and balances. If individuals of a given species are continually squeezed out into unfavorable habitat, or if they need the company of their own kind to survive, territorial defense on the part of the stronger birds can be damaging.

Incidentally, the selection of a territory is not always the best available. Some species, because of their strong homing instincts, will persist in occupying a certain spot even though the habitat has deteriorated. Recently, an office co-worker showed me the nest of a Horned Lark near the front door of a post office. The latter, a new building, had been constructed on a piece of farm land where the birds had been nesting for years.

In Africa, where endless variety appears to be the order of the day, many species live in harmony because their food habits differ. Conversely, if their food habits are similar, the species involved often occupy different habitats. In our country also, we have birds in both categories.

That birds defend their nesting territories is not new to science. Aristotle wrote of it many years ago.

Courtship

The male House Wren is in his nesting territory when courtship time arrives. In my experience, the females show up for the first time after the male has built, in rough form, one or more nests. On the other hand, as mentioned before, some ducks appear on their nesting grounds already paired. In their case, a part of the courtship activity is over. From these examples, we see that courtship can take place in more than one part of the range.

Pectoral Sandpiper, *Calidris melanotos.* In this species, the upper breast is darkly streaked and abruptly set off from the pale belly, but this is not the full story. On the breeding grounds, the male throws out his chest conspicuously when he calls. This temporary protrusion is unusual among birds. During migration, about all we hear is a weak *kriek* call. 23 cm. (9″)

House Wren, *Troglodytes aedon.* When experimenting with houses for this species, I found that a male wren, upon arriving in spring, would fill all the nearby houses with sticks, apparently with the expectation that many females would come along to use them. The females that came demonstrated their liking for a nest by adding the soft lining to the roughly built foundation as provided by the male. 13 cm. (5″)

Red-breasted Nuthatch, *Sitta canadensis.* (female) The nest cavity, which has the same general appearance as that of our woodpeckers, and which the nuthatch often constructs itself, is usually well plastered around the entrance door with resin, a transparent substance obtained from pine or fir trees. The nesting range, which is vast, is not entirely vacated in winter, although many birds move southward. 11 cm. (4.5")

Ruby-throated Hummingbird, *Archilochus colubris.* (female) The female hummingbird builds her nest often in open woodlands, preferably in the lower story where there will be shelter from above. Normally, it is saddled on a small branch rather than placed in a crotch. It will not be easily seen, though, as the birds camouflage the nest with lichens. Two eggs will be laid. 9 cm. (3.5")

When a male Northern Cardinal offers food to his mate or to a prospective mate, we say he is courting. When a Wild Turkey spreads his tail in the presence of his hens, we say he is engaged in a courtship ritual. When both members of a pair of birds sing antiphonally, we say they are communicating. We speak of these actions as though the birds were human.

Not all activities on the part of males are easy to categorize, however. What is the meaning of the "sky dances" of such species as the American Woodcock and the Common Snipe? Are they a part of courtship, or of territorial defense, or of both? What about the fantastic manner in which Western Grebes run across the surface of the water? Does this have more than one meaning?

In some species, the female takes the lead in courtship. I think of the phalaropes in this connection.

Among our birds there are species that remain mated for only one season or part thereof, some that remain mated throughout the year (or for several years), and others that apparently mate only at intervals of two or more years. Some species are regularly promiscuous. Thus seasons of courtship vary with the species.

Nest Sites

During my grammar school days, an egg-collector reached down into the chimney on the house next door and pulled out the nest and eggs of a Chimney Swift. (This was during the period when egg-collecting was still in vogue.) I was impressed by the bird's choice of location. Very few enemies could get to the nest there. Even the egg-collector had a difficult time of it.

When hiding their nests in trees, some species go a step further and cover them with lichens, moss, and other delicate materials, apparently in an effort to camouflage them. Many species of birds strive to hide their nests.

On the other hand, certain species make no effort at all in this direction. The Osprey, for example, will construct its nest in the top of a dead tree. And the Canada Goose, when she builds her nest on top of a muskrat house, indicates that she does not need vegetative cover. She depends upon the gander to defend the nest. The Killdeer nests on the open ground with no protection whatsoever for its eggs, except that they are not easily seen. Ring-billed Gulls and other birds that nest on the ground in colonies, apparently have a great deal to gain by sticking together. If an enemy attacks the colony, it generally gets the eggs or chicks around the edges. The larger the colony, the better are the chances for the occupants in the center to survive.

Several years ago, I had a Red-winged Blackbird's nest under observation. It was attached to four or five reeds. After a few days, some of the reeds grew taller than the others with the result that the nest was tipped. Thus the vegetation played a trick on the birds.

Those species that nest in cavities have the advantage. Protection is relatively good, and the nestlings are more or less forced to remain in their nests until they are ready to fly. The young birds most subject to ground predation are those that run about shortly after hatching.

When birds have more than one brood per season, the nest site for the second or third brood may differ from that used for the first brood. Plant growth and temperature changes may be partly responsible for this. In some species, the males play a part in selecting the nest site, but in others the female assumes the responsibility.

Osprey, *Pandion haliaetus.* The Osprey shown here was in the process of constructing its nest when I took its picture. The tree selected was dead. In those areas where there are no dead trees, Ospreys sometimes build their nests atop utility poles. Thus wildlife managers have begun a system of providing special poles with platforms built on them. 58cm. (23″)

Eggs of Killdeer, *Charadrius vociferus.* As is widely known, Killdeer do not construct a nest. They simply lay their eggs on the ground, often among gravel. Apparently the spotting on the eggs renders them inconspicuous, for the birds are well able to maintain their numbers. One thing in their favor is their habit of nesting afar from water, as well as near it.

American Goldfinch, *Carduelis tristis.* (female) To see flocks of goldfinches feeding on dandelion seeds on our lawns is a common sight. When thus engaged, we might wonder why they are not busy with their nesting chores. Well, in many parts of their range, they are late nesters. In the Great Lakes region, for example, eggs may not be laid until early July. 13 cm. (5")

Red-winged Blackbird, *Agelaius phoeniceus.* (female) Changes in wildlife habitat, caused by man's activities, have been detrimental to many species of birds, but this apparently has not been the case with the Red-winged Blackbird. It prefers to nest in our wetlands, it seems, but when necessary, it will nest in our uplands. The female, shown here, is smaller than the male, and her calls are different. 19 cm. (7.5")

Nests

I remember an instance when I had bluebird houses in my yard, wherein a pair (the male accompanied the female) of Eastern Bluebirds began to build their nest early in March. The weather was warm and springlike. Then came three weeks of cold weather. The bluebirds discontinued their work until late March when normal spring weather returned. From this, I concluded that weather conditions have a bearing, perhaps indirectly, upon the nesting calendar of the bluebird. It was not the whole story, for late March was the average starting time for them in my yard. It seems that most species can be counted on to follow a consistent nesting calendar.

In the case of the Eastern Bluebird, the female constructs the nest. I have seen males with dry grass in their bills, but I am sure that such activity is nothing more than a sign of exuberance on their part. This, of course, is not the case throughout the bird world, for, in some species the males may either assist with nest building or do virtually all of it.

It is amazing how consistent the birds of a given species can be in nest construction. A careful observer can recognize a nest by its form and by the material used. Thus the Ovenbird, in keeping with its name, constructs its nest with an opening in the side. The House Wren constructs its nest mainly of dry sticks. The nest of the Red-eyed Vireo is securely anchored to a forked branch. The Mourning Dove constructs a frail nest through which the eggs can be seen.

Not all species construct their own nests. Many species of owls, for example, will make use of old nests built by other creatures. Cavity-nesters of various species often take over the old nest sites of woodpeckers.

Among many species, particularly our smaller ones, the standard procedure is to build the nest foundation of rough materials, and line it with finer or softer things. Such nests are completed before the eggs are laid. Among waterfowl, there are ducks that add to their nests after the eggs are laid. Some hawks do this, also, but probably for a different reason. The goldfinch may add two or more stories to its nest when cowbird eggs are imposed upon it.

Many species build one nest for the first brood and, if their first attempt is thwarted, a second nest. Those species that normally raise two or more broods per season may construct a new nest for each brood. Some do not, but there are a number of advantages in starting out anew. Most of the nests I have seen are pretty well trampled out of shape by the time the nestlings leave. Some species, especially if they are polygamous, build several nests at the outset. When the male House Wren fills several bird houses with sticks at the start of the breeding season, he is hopeful that several females will come along to occupy them. On the other hand, I have seen male House Wrens which had but one mate industriously feeding the nestlings as though he were monogamous.

Most birds construct nests for their own use, but there are exceptions. The Groove-billed Ani, for example, is one species wherein more than one pair may be observed working on the same nest. Some ducks regularly lay their eggs in the nests of other ducks. Wildlife managers call these nests "dump nests."

Eggs

I can remember the first nest of eggs I ever saw. I was in the second grade at the time and the neighbor's children showed it to me. It was a Gray Catbird's nest with three eggs. I can still see in my mind's eye the rich blue-green color of those eggs. I can also realize why

Ovenbird, *Seiurus aurocapillus.* As indicated in the name, Ovenbirds build their nests like an oven with the entrance in the side. These are built on the forest floor, but in situations where there is some camouflage. It is not necessary to go to the forests to see this warbler, however. I notice that it visits our flower gardens quite regularly during migration. 15 cm. (6")

Yellow Warbler, *Dendroica petechia.* (female) The Yellow Warbler is a common victim of the cowbird. Sometimes it builds a second story over its nest to cover the unwanted eggs, but this may also include some of its own eggs. The nesting range of the Yellow Warbler is far-reaching, extending from southern Mexico and vicinity, to the arctic tundra, except for minor gaps. 13 cm. (5")

Golden-crowned Kinglet, *Regulus satrapa.* (female) Golden-crowned Kinglets can be observed in either coniferous or deciduous growth, but they seem to prefer coniferous, particularly spruce, for nesting purposes. Surprisingly, this species may lay as many as eight or nine eggs to the set. The female incubates them, but the male assists in feeding the young. 10 cm. (4")

Eggs of the American Woodcock, *Scolopax minor.* The eggs are dark in color, so they do not stand out very prominently when the bird is away. They are simply laid in a leaf-lined depression in the soil. The chicks are precocial, but it takes them a few days to grow strong. The nesting range extends from Newfoundland and Florida on the east, to southern Manitoba and eastern Texas on the west.

early day ornithologists were so intrigued with egg-collecting.

Egg clutch-size may range from one to more than one dozen eggs. Waterfowl are among those species that lay the larger sets. The California Condor is an example of a species that lays but one egg. Most song birds are in between. The Black-throated Gray Warbler, for example, lays three to five eggs. If a species lays more than one clutch per season, the second or third set may contain fewer eggs than the first. In some species, the more northerly populations may lay more eggs per clutch than their southern counterparts. There are instances, though, when extremely cold temperatures may inhibit laying.

Not all species reach maturity within the same number of months. Some species lay eggs for the first time at the age of two or more years. The majority of species do lay eggs, though, during the first nesting season following their natal year. The usual expectation is that one egg will be laid each day, but some species, especially our larger ones, lay their eggs at intervals of two or more days.

That dull-colored or spotted eggs are less likely to be seen by the bird's enemies than white eggs is no doubt true. Some species that lay white or nearly white eggs seem to realize this, for they cover their eggs with debris while away from the nest. Ducks commonly do this. Cavity-nesters that lay white eggs have built-in protection for their pale eggs. Those birds whose chicks run about shortly after hatching lay proportionally larger eggs than those whose chicks grow up in the nest.

In some species, the eggs have a glossy finish; in others a dull finish. Occasionally, this distinction is useful for identification purposes. Shapes vary, some species laying eggs that are sharply pointed. Other species lay eggs that are nearly spherical in shape. Color, in conjunction with shape, helps to identify most eggs. Spotting, though a help, can be quite variable in pattern as well as in color. Occasionally, albinic eggs are laid. When all else fails and size must be relied upon, the most reliable dimension of an egg is its breadth.

Egg-laying dates are more precise and dependable than nesting dates for research purposes.

Incubation Periods

Many song birds can hatch their eggs in somewhat less than two weeks. Larger birds, in many cases, require more time. The females, with certain exceptions, bear the brunt of the work load. Most are reluctant to leave their nests when disturbed. In those cases where the males assist the females, the latter generally take the night shift, and often certain parts of the day shift as well. The situation is different with the phalaropes and certain other species, however, for with them the males bear the responsibility of hatching the eggs.

The parents turn the eggs regularly while incubating, but the chicks, when they are ready to hatch, break the egg shells with their bills. In some cases, the parents carry the egg shells away; in others, they eat them.

Some species start to incubate as soon as the first egg is laid, some after two or three are laid, and others after the set has been completed. It may be that the eggs are safer when covered from the first day, and some species do start in this way, with the result that the nestlings vary in size.

If the species is precocial (meaning that the chicks leave the nest shortly after hatching), it is advantageous to have all of them hatch at the same time. Many such species do delay the start of incubation until all eggs are laid.

Rose-breasted Grosbeak, *Pheucticus ludovicianus.* (female) Nests of this species are built often in trees and shrubs. They are not strong in construction, but they seem to serve well as the species is able to maintain its numbers. The males assist with incubation as well as with the feeding of the young. Surprisingly, they sing while incubating. This is a *no-no* among most species. 20 cm. (8")

Gray Catbird, *Dumetella carolinensis.* I first became acquainted with the Gray Catbird when I was eight years of age. I shall never forget it, for, as I was peering into its nest, one of the parent birds flew repeatedly at my head, while wailing at the top of its voice. (This was not its usual catlike *meow,* for which the species is named.) 23 cm. (9")

Royal Tern, *Sterna maxima.* Most terns nest in colonies, but this species carries the custom to the extreme. The clutches of eggs (no nest) are situated so closely to one another on the ground, that the incubating birds cannot fly to and from them without striking their neighbors with their wings. Nevertheless, the birds and their chicks can recognize one another without difficultly. 51 cm. (20″)

Cedar Waxwing, *Bombycilla cedrorum.* Waxwings build their nests in both coniferous and deciduous trees, the males assisting the females. Incubation of the eggs is performed by the female, but the male assists with the feeding of the young. The immature, shown here, has streaks in its plumage. (Photographed in September.) 18 cm. (7″)

Earlier in this chapter, we mentioned that some species of ducks regularly lay their eggs in the nests of other ducks. If they lay them well after the rightful mother has started to incubate, we may assume that such eggs will not be hatched, for the mother will have to leave the nest when her own eggs hatch in order to take care of her chicks.

The majority of birds remain quiet while incubating their eggs, apparently for the sake of safety. Surprisingly, some species such as the Rose-breasted Grosbeak and certain vireos sing while on the nest. Many species become excited and noisy if the nest is attacked, but this is a different matter.

During the incubation period, some species have bare spots, called brood patches, on their bodies which permit the eggs to come into direct contact with the skin. Usually, it is the female that is so equipped, but in certain species the males have these patches. It is interesting to note that some sea birds warm their eggs with their feet.

We have mentioned that the Canada Goose has a very attentive and strong gander to assist in defending the nest. The same system prevails among many song birds, and the males may bring food to the females as well. In those cases when males exchange incubation periods with females, there may be a sort of ritual, including calls and motions.

When researchers need the actual length of the incubation period, they can obtain it best by marking the eggs as they are laid. Having determined the date on which the final egg was laid, they can watch to see when it hatches. The time span of the final egg is the most accurate. If a researcher compares the incubation periods of a given species for several years, he may find some variation, for weather conditions, the size of the clutch, whether the incubating bird was unduly disturbed, and other factors, may exert their influence. Also, it is known that some species may not start to incubate immediately after the final egg is laid.

If there is no pollution such as that caused by chemical sprays, and the bird's natural enemies keep their distance, a good hatch can be expected. The parent birds, in most species, stick to their tasks quite faithfully, and it is seldom that the eggs are naturally sterile. Occasionally, cold temperatures may be fatal, especially during the late stages of incubation. Certain species may desert their eggs if disturbed by man.

Care Of The Young

While taking a bird count one day in May, my party flushed a young Great Horned Owl. It flew to a slender branch high in a tree. Upon landing, it plunged heavily forward and swung head downward. It hung there like a sloth for a few minutes, and we wondered whether it could right itself. When we walked over to investigate, it dropped down into the air, righted itself, and flew away. This showed me that although young birds are awkward, they can and do get along.

Young birds are most vulnerable immediately after hatching. The parents are extra diligent during this period and may brood them all night as well as during parts of the day. Many altricial species (birds whose newly hatched young are helpless and hence confined to the nest for some time) brood their young until they are nearly ready to leave the nest. Among precocial species, some parents brood their young in the usual way (on the ground); others allow their chicks to climb upon their backs. The Horned Grebe is an example of the latter.

Methods of feeding the young vary considerably.

Canada Goose, *Branta canadensis.* For the most part, Canada Geese are well able to maintain their numbers. One thing that helps in this respect is their determination and ability to defend their nests. The ganders, in particular, excel in this way, and can rear the broods alone if their mates are killed. (Shown here is a female and goslings.) 99 cm. (39″)

Wood Duck, *Aix sponsa.* (female) The female is grayish-brown in general color, but mottled on the breast and sides. It is her habit to hatch her chicks within tree cavities, often at considerable heights above the ground, so the question arises as to how she gets them down safely. She calls them down when they are old enough, and the fall to the ground does not injure them. 48 cm. (19″)

Nest of Great Horned Owl, *Bubo virgianus.* Here we see the young of the Great Horned Owl in a nest that was built probably by a hawk. The location is an abandoned farm in Kansas. From this example, we can see that Great Horned Owls, normally residents of the forests, will make do with whatever they can find.

American Avocet, *Recurvirostra americana.* Although avocets winter in small numbers as far east as Florida, they are birds of the West during the nesting season. I obtained my picture in Saskatchewan, which is on the northern edge of the range. As indicated here, avocets are colonial during the breeding season. They lay their eggs virtually on the ground, for they do not construct a nest in the usual sense. 46cm. (18")

Hummingbirds feed their nestlings by regurgitation. Most altricial species simply deposit morsels of food in the throats of the young. Some, such as the hawks, deposit items of food at the edge of the nest for the nestlings to pick up. Among the precocial species, we find parents that feed their young, some that assist their young in locating food, and others that allow their young to find their own food. The young of smaller species, especially those that feed on insects, need food at frequent intervals. Those of our larger species can wait fairly long, because they usually receive generous servings at one time. The young of seed-eating birds often are fed insects at first.

Most species maintain a consistent schedule when caring for their young, some even risking danger to themselves while thus engaged. Most species care for their young until they are well able to fly, but there are exceptions. The Purple Martin, for example, when it feels the urge to migrate southward, may abandon its young even though they are still in the nest.

Anyone who has tried to pick up a young robin knows how excited a parent bird can become. With few exceptions, the parents keep a careful watch over their young, both in and out of the nest. Some species will actually attack the enemy, while others will put on a broken-wing act or other sign of distress in an effort to entice the enemy away from the young. The young are often very proficient at doing their part too. They know when to be quiet, when to lie still, and when to run to their parents.

In many species, the female gets the brunt of the work connected with the care of the young. In a few, the male has the responsibility. In others, the two parents may divide the work about equally. There are cases in which the male cares for the young of the first brood, while the female starts the second brood. Occasionally, the young of the first brood assist with the feeding of the second brood. Normally, birds feed only their own progeny, but if a parent loses its young, it may feed those of almost any species, even against the protests of the rightful parents. Among waterfowl, ducklings of one brood may mingle with those of another brood without hostility on the part of the parents.

The young of certain species are reluctant to leave their nests, even when they are old enough. The parents have to push them out. This is in contrast to those that insist upon getting out before they are able to fly. Nest sanitation is important among many of our song birds, but not among certain of our larger species. Eventually, the young do learn to find their own food and shelter. How much is instinct and how much is learned from their parents is debatable. Banding records show that many shorebirds leave their arctic nesting grounds ahead of their young. The latter must have some innate ability, for they migrate to their winter quarters at a later date.

Researchers find that in some species (if not all), they can imprint themselves upon the young birds as though they were their "foster parents." Of course, this has to be done at an early age or it will not work. What then is the situation with the young cowbird? Is it not imprinted upon a foster parent? And yet it joins flocks of its own species as soon as it is able to take care of itself. How does it recognize them?

Length Of The Nesting Cycle

In northern latitudes, a given species may rear one brood, while in southern latitudes the same species may rear two or three. Some species, limited to the arctic regions, rear one brood annually; other species, living in

Indigo Bunting, *Passerina cyanea* (male) In my experience, the Indigo Bunting is a favorite among bird observers. One of the reasons for this is the fact that the males sing throughout most of the summer and during the heat of the day. As they sing often from high perches, with the sky as the background, they may appear to be black in color. 14cm. (5.5″)

White-throated Sparrow, *Zonotrichia albicollis. Old Sam Peabody, Peabody, Peabody,* the New England version of this sparrow's song, has stayed with me throughout my life. I like the bird's dooryard ways too. Nothing can be more pleasant than to have a flock of them in the back yard, no matter what the season. In Virginia, during the fall, I enjoyed their rally calls as they went to roost at night. 18cm. (7″)

Bobolink, *Dolichonyx oryzivorus.* (male) What a feeling of reckless abandon the Bobolink expresses while singing on the wing! Poets have taken up the theme and written at length about it. Included in some of this poetry have been allusions to the bird's name, Bob-o-link, which it is thought, may be short for Robert of Lincoln. 18cm. (7″)

Hermit Thrush, *Catharus guttatus.* The song of the Hermit Thrust is considered by many listeners to be one of the best, if not the best, in the bird world. From the musical standpoint, it is a model. The tones are pure, the phrases are varied, and the concert usually rendered is long enough to make a profound impression upon the listener. 18cm. (7″)

a warmer climate, may rear but one brood as well. Some species, especially the larger ones, require more time for incubation of the eggs and fledging of the young than others. A few species may rear three or four broods annually. Thus the length of the nesting cycle varies with the species.

Bird Song

When I lived in St. Louis many years ago, I heard an excellent program of bird-song imitations by a nationally known artist. This was before bird songs were recorded mechanically, so the artist whistled most of the songs. After giving the program, he evaluated his efforts and told us, facetiously, how a certain elderly person responded to them. This person exclaimed that she enjoyed the program very much and was sure that she could now recognize the call of the *Whip-poor-will!* This remark only served to underscore the value of his program, for the audience, a capacity crowd, immediately gave him a hearty round of applause.

The fact that the above program was so well attended demonstrated to me that there was a lot of interest in bird songs. Today, we see a similar interest when tape recorders are taken out into the field. If there were no bird songs, I believe mankind would be greatly impoverished. In spring, when hopes of better things to come arise in the heart of man, it seems the songs of birds add the final touch. In summer, their tranquil melodies give us a feeling of serenity. In autumn, their songs, often muted, assure us that all is not lost. And in winter, their songs, often fragmented at this time, remind us that spring is on its way.

Bird songs appeal to ornithologists for several reasons, one of which is utilitarian. When bird counts are made, almost ninety percent of the species encountered are identified by their songs or calls. Certainly many of the birds would be missed entirely if they did not have the ability to call. Some species make their songs more appealing by alternating between two or more types; the Northern Cardinal is well known for this. A few species, such as the Carolina Wren, may sing antiphonally.

Quality Of The Song

When we speak of bird song, we commonly think of small birds. Some large birds can make musical sounds also, but we frequently describe their efforts as "calls." Many species have both songs and calls in their repertoire. Birds are able to sing because they have a syrinx, a vocal organ located well down in the windpipe. Its structure is not the same in all species, and it is totally lacking in vultures. Certain nonvocal sounds serve the same purpose as songs. The drumming (vibration of the wings) of the Ruffed Grouse is an example.

Any bird can be depended upon to sing *its* song. Most species do this so well that humans normally cannot detect any variations. Recording devices, though, demonstrate that there may be minor variations between any two individuals of the same species, and even in the songs of the individual itself. The most pronounced variations arise when the birds are widely separated geographically. Closely related races may have either similar or different song patterns.

Not every listener can hear the songs of some species. High-pitched songs are the most difficult in this respect. On the other hand, some people cannot hear the low-pitched songs. Listeners, as a result of these problems, may hear only parts of songs. To avoid this difficultly, some birders record the songs on tape and

Vesper Sparrow, *Pooecetes gramineus.* The Vesper Sparrow has won for itself a very appropriate name, for its song is in keeping with the relaxed atmosphere of the late evening. Sometimes two or more birds may be heard singing at the same time in their respective territories, for the sound carries well at this hour. 15 cm. (6″)

Fox Sparrow, *Passerella iliaca.* The trees were laden with freshly-fallen snow. It looked like Christmas! The Fox Sparrows seemed to be everywhere; and they were singing. What a concert! And this was only March. Thus, I found them while working in northern Wisconsin. We have several forms of this species and they vary in color geographically. (My photograph was taken in Wisconsin.) 18 cm. (7″)

Field Sparrow, *Spizella pusilla.* Abandoned fields where there are a few clumps of bushes and one or two trees are the favorite haunts of the Field Sparrow. The trees serve as song perches, and the bushes as nest sites, although nests are built frequently on the ground. Field Sparrows are renowned singers. It is during the summer that their songs are most appreciated. 14cm. (5.5")

Brown Creeper, *Certhia americana.* While checking deer yards in northern Wisconsin, I occasionally heard the song of the Brown Creeper. It reminded me of the song of the Louisiana Waterthrush, although it was weak by comparison. Northern Wisconsin is within the breeding range of the Brown Creeper, it is important to note, as the birds do not sing very often in their winter range. 14cm. (5.5")

play them back with the volume louder than usual.

When bird songs are imitated in the field, we normally suspect the Northern Mockingbird. Imagine my surprise therefore, when I heard the song of the Western Meadowlark one day, and looked up to see the Chestnut-collared Longspur. Another unexpected imitation is the call of the Greater Yellowlegs as rendered by the Pine Grosbeak, especially when there is snow on the ground. Normally these grosbeaks are so quiet at this time, that many people call them "mopes."

When Do Birds Sing?

Light intensity appears to be a strong factor in the singing of many species. Those observers who take part in the annual Breeding Bird Survey know this only too well, for they are required to start out by the clock. If clouds are heavy at this hour, singing may be delayed. I notice also that deep shade in a forest will delay singing there. Conversely, in the evening, it seems that whip-poor-wills, for example, may call earlier in the deep shade than in habitat that is more open. Not every species reacts to the intensity of light in the same way. The Northern Mockingbird sings during the night, while the Barred Owl hoots during the day. In migration, many diurnal species call at night.

Temperature plays an important role in the timing of bird song. Many species that seldom sing during the winter months in northern latitudes sing regularly during this season in southern latitudes. In either latitude singing slows down during the heat of the day and during the heat of the summer. Some species refrain from singing while they are outside their breeding range.

Where Do Birds Sing?

Many species have their favorite song perches. Photographers know this and frequently secure good pictures there by setting up their cameras in advance. Some species, such as the Northern Mockingbird, sing from conspicuous perches; other species do the opposite, as though they were afraid of being seen. Many species such as the warblers sing while they are searching for food among the branches of trees; others take time out to sing. A rather large number of species sing regularly in flight.

Why Do Birds Sing?

To answer this question completely presents a real challenge. Birds in general sing so vigorously and so regularly during the start of the nesting season, that song must be closely linked to courtship activities and the establishment of the home. It is perfectly synchronized with the bird's physical condition at this time. As many species sing also during the nonbreeding season, we can assume that birds have more than one reason for singing.

Previously, I mentioned that birds employ both songs and calls in their daily living. Certain birds, like the bushtits and chickadees, apparently, use short calls as a means of keeping the flock together. Another use for short calls may be to warn companions of approaching danger. Crows seem to employ this use. Whether birds sing because they are happy is often debated. It seems that some species do.

Migration

The subject of migration is one of the most intriguing in the science of ornithology. How do the birds find their way? How do they know when to start

Killdeer, *Charadrius vociferus.* To those of us who live in the North, the first call of the Killdeer is a welcome sign of spring. Often this call is heard while the bird is still on the wing. The Killdeer differs from many of our plovers in that it can live in a variety of habitats, both wet and dry. 25 cm. (10″)

Red-winged Blackbird, *Agelaius phoeniceus.* (male) In the North, the song of the Red-winged Blackbird, coming as it does on the heels of winter, strikes a responsive chord as it rings out over the frozen marshes. Whether it is the song of a lone male, or the tinkling chorus of a flock of them in a tree, it comes as a sign of approaching spring. 22 cm. (8.5″)

Song Sparrow, *Melospiza melodia.* The Song Sparrow brings hope and cheer to thousands of people every spring as it moves northward on the heels of winter. It seems to be ever ready to sing; and its song can be recognized throughout our land even though there are many geographical forms. When singing, the bird is often on a conspicuous perch. (My picture was taken in the Midwest.) 15 cm. (6")

Eastern Phoebe, *Sayornis phoebe.* In the northern parts of its range, this phoebe is a welcome sign of spring. It comes as soon as insect life can be found in the vicinity of water. It is a mouse-colored bird which can best be recognized by its tail-wagging habit (if it is not calling). The young have two wingbars. 18 cm. (7")

out? Why do some leave an abundant food supply and fly to the Arctic where food is relatively scarce? Why do some individuals of a given species migrate while others remain behind? Answers have been slow in coming to these and similar questions, but perhaps that is why the subject is so alluring.

Only in recent years have we learned that certain species can become torpid during the winter. The Common Poorwill is one example.[1] Not many species do this, but prior to this discovery such a thing would have seemed incredible.

It has been estimated that the spring season travels northward at the rate of 24 kilometers (15 mi.) per day. Obviously, birds can migrate much faster than this. Canada Geese and certain species of ducks seem to be very impatient to reach their breeding grounds, for they press forward as fast as the ice melts on the rivers and marshes. Other species proceed slowly, as though waiting for the spring season to get a good start, and speed up later as they approach their nesting grounds.

When I lived in Missouri, I kept spring arrival dates for as many species as I could. When I moved to Wisconsin, I did the same thing. Then I noticed that in some species the dates were about the same for the two locations. This led me to believe that some species may "put down" simultaneously over a vast area.

The regularity with which the majority of species arrive is phenomenal. In some species, this holds true even though the season is backward. One morning during the migration period of Swainson's Thrush, I was walking toward my office when an individual of this species attempted to get out of my way. It could fly but

1. E.C. Jaeger, "Further observations on the hibernation of the Poorwill," *Condor,* 51:105-109, 1949.

a short distance. Suspecting that the bird was benumbed by the cold temperature, I took it into my office. After a very short time, it was thawed out and ready to be on its way. Although a given species may arrive punctually, not all of the population hangs together. The birds will be "strung out" for many days, and this is in their favor. Adverse weather, if it gets some of them, will not get the entire population.

Migration in the fall is often associated with the passage of a cold front. We find birds in great numbers shortly after such a passage. This does not apply to all species. Some appear to be in such a rush to move southward that they even leave their young behind. Some flycatchers do this, and many shorebirds are notorious for leaving their young to find their own way. On the other hand, Canada Geese regularly migrate as family groups, and among song birds, the same can be said for some of the warblers.

A peculiarity of herons and of some ducks is their proclivity to migrate northward in late summer before starting southward for the winter. Certain other species depart for the South in August, well in advance of the influence of cold temperatures. Is day's length a factor?

The urge to migrate is strong in most species, yet some can be easily persuaded to linger to the north of their usual wintering grounds. Refuge areas provided for geese regularly waylay large numbers of these birds, much to the disappointment of sportsmen to the south. The same thing happens among song birds, occasionally, when food is provided especially for them.

Waterfowl (as well as many other species) migrate north and south so consistently that wildlife managers now recognize four principal flyways in North America. These are the Atlantic, Mississippi, Central, and Pacific flyways. (The Central flyway lies in the Great Plains.) Not

Rose-breasted Grosbeak, *Pheucticus ludovicianus.* (male) The song of this grosbeak is rhythmical and pleasing to the ear. It is softer and more continuous than that of the robin, with which it is often compared. The *crick* call is also distinctive. Sometimes this is the only note we hear, especially when the birds first arrive. It is not unusual at this time to see several males sitting quietly in the same tree-top, as though they all had come at once and needed to look over the situation before proceding farther. 20 cm. (8″)

Northern Oriole, *Icterus galbula.* The oriole illustrated here appears to be a first-year male of the *Baltimore* form. It is predominately yellow instead of orange. (I took the picture in early June.) 19 cm. (7.5″)

Palm Warbler, *Dendroica palmarum.* In Wisconsin, we look for this warbler about the time when the wild plum thickets come into bloom. The flying insects that commonly gather in these thickets may be the attraction. We recognize the warbler by its habit of continuously pumping its tail. Its song may be described as a series of four to six dry notes, all on about the same pitch. 13 cm. (5")

Red-breasted Nuthatch, *Sitta canadensis.* (male) This species is our only nuthatch that is strongly migratory. In fact, many people think of it only as a winter visitor, for its breeding range is restricted rather closely to our colder regions. It does not come in the same numbers each year, but is cyclic. In my experience, it shows a preference for conifers. 11 cm. (4.5")

all species follow these patterns. The Tundra Swans (formerly called "whistling") that winter in Chesapeake Bay, for example, migrate northward by way of Wisconsin and neighboring states. Thus they have an east-west migration route for a part of the way. The Lesser Golden Plover (formerly called American) commonly migrates northward by way of the Mississippi flyway in spring and southward across the Atlantic Ocean in the fall.

If birds use certain routes consistently, as they seem to do, how do they find their way? Much effort has been spent by researchers to answer this question. Some species follow the seacoasts, while others traverse the interior where there are no visible guidelines. Birds often migrate on cloudy nights, so it is thought that at least some species are guided by the earth's magnetic field.

Although most birds accurately follow their ancestral routes, certain individuals may be thrown off course without apparent reason. For example, stray warblers of eastern species show up, on occasion, west of the Rocky Mountains. Similarly, birds, while enroute, may show up in habitat that seems to be entirely unsuited to them. Only last year, I found a Dickcissel in song, on an exceptionally early date, in the business section of a northern city.

It has been estimated that approximately half of our species cross the latitudinal line of the Rio Grande during the spring and fall seasons. Some of these migrate well down into South America. In addition to these, we have birds migrating to and from Asia, Europe, Africa, and Australia, and some of these breed in the Southern Hemisphere. In North America, some form of migration can be witnessed during any month of the year.

It is interesting to speculate which end of the

migration route should be called *home*. Some observers believe that home is where the nest is built. Others take the opposite view. Banding experiments show that certain species "home" to their winter quarters just as consistently as elsewhere.

The subject of migration is further complicated because only part of the population of some species migrates in a given year. I have observed this in the Blue Jay. Other species, such as the Eastern Bluebird, migrate to the southern portion of their breeding range. The Snowy Owl moves southward irregularly, apparently only when food is scarce on its breeding grounds. Certain species that nest in the high mountains may migrate to the lowlands for the winter. In spring, some birds migrate northward as a species, large flocks being found in one tree. Others, like some species of ducks, travel to their breeding grounds in pairs. In still other species the males migrate first. During migration peaks many species travel together.

Birds migrate at various altitudes depending upon a number of factors. Occasionally aviators check them at tremendous heights, but this is exceptional. It seems that the majority, even in fair weather, do not exceed 0.8 kilometers (½ mi.). In adverse weather, large numbers of small birds strike tall objects such as television towers at night, so it is apparent that they migrate at low altitudes during such weather. The Wood Thrush migrates entirely at night, while others, such as the swallows, migrate by day. Canada Geese migrate at either time.

Winds of moderate velocity are helpful, not to blow the birds, but to give them uplift. Crosswinds do not seem to be a hinderance. Unusual winds may blow migrants off their course. Sometimes birds are grounded from exhaustion during stormy weather. Prolonged rain

Tundra Swan, *Cygnus columbianus.* The Tundra Swan, formerly called the Whistling Swan, is our most widely distributed and best-known swan. At close range, a small, yellow spot may be seen on the dark area in front of the eye in some (not all) specimens. Immatures are grayish, especially on the head and neck, and have pinkish bills. 135cm. (53")

Yellow-crowned Night-Heron, *Nycticorax violaceus.* We commonly think of this heron as a bird of the subtropical regions, and so it is, but it migrates northward along the waterways of our eastern states (U.S.) as far as the latitude of Wisconsin. I have observed it here, and feeding during the day, at that. 63cm. (25")

Blackburnian Warbler, *Dendroica fusca.* I took this photograph early in October, in Wisconsin. The bird did not call, but it appears to be an immature Blackburnian Warbler. This species starts out for its winter quarters in Central America and northern South America sometime in August, but many individuals linger in our country until the end of October. 13 cm. (5")

Bobolink, *Dolichonyx oryzivorus.* The Bobolink shown here appears to be a young male. I took the picture during July, in Wisconsin. 18 cm. (7")

in spring can help the observer, though, for it brings the insects down close to the ground. The birds, in turn, descend for the insects, where they can be easily observed. On the other hand, if fair weather prevails for long periods of time, very few song birds may be seen, for they simply fly overhead without stopping.

Today researchers use radar, radio transmitters, and airplanes, in addition to laboratory experiments, bird banding, and scanning of the moon with telescopes in order to learn more about migration. When information is sought as to why or how the birds do what they do, we find that those things that apply to one species may not necessarily apply to all.

Food Habits

Late one evening, while watching my bird feeder, I noticed that a male Northern Cardinal was busy feeding his mate. He was taking sunflower seeds to her, but before flying to the shrub where she was perched, he was careful to remove the hull from the seed. This he did with his bill. The Blue Jay also eats sunflower seeds but lacks the muscular equipment of the cardinal. It takes the seed to a perch where it can hold it tightly with its toes. Then with two or three blows of its bill, it extracts the kernel.

The Loggerhead Shrike cannot catch or hold its prey with its feet, but it knows how to snag it on a thorn or on a barbed-wire fence. When I was in grammar school, I had an opportunity to walk regularly along such a fence. I found grasshoppers most often, and they were always snagged through the thorax with their bellies up. The shrikes lined up more food than they needed.

Owls can hold their prey in their claws or carry it in their bills if they so desire. They also have the ability to transfer food to their mouths by simply raising a foot. In this way, they differ from the hawks, which normally bend down to tear off a bit of food.

Many species of birds disgorge indigestible matter, but hawks and owls are especially notable in this respect. Owls commonly swallow their food whole and disgorge at least one pellet per day as a rule. Hawks disgorge pellets somewhat less often. Researchers get a general idea of the diet of certain owls by analyzing pellets which they find near their roosts. Bones and fur of mammals, for example, can be identified. They also watch the owls to see what they catch, as pellets do not tell the complete story. For example, if two creatures are represented in the pellets, one of them may have been in the stomach of the other; or, the hair of the prey species may not "ball" and be disgorged; or, the pellet picked up for analysis may have been disgorged by an owl other than those believed to be using the roost under study. As hawks reject certain parts of their prey, and digest what they eat rather thoroughly, their pellets serve to tell only a part of the story.

A similar problem exists when studies are made of bird stomachs. The food contents of stomachs have been analyzed systematically by various agencies in North America since the early 1880's. But, as certain food items do not show up at this stage of digestion, such studies are incomplete, and need to be supplemented by observations in the field.

One day while in Texas, I watched a Reddish Egret twirling around and stamping its feet as though it had lost its balance. It then proceeded to pick up an item of food. What a contrast, I thought, to the method used by the Green-backed Heron (formerly Green Heron). The latter often sits calmly at the edge of the water until something edible comes along. A few days later, I had an opportunity to study the feeding habits of the Cattle

Reddish Egret, *Egretta rufescens.* One day while attempting to photograph water birds, I saw a Reddish Egret jumping in the water as though it had a hot foot. A bit later, it ran for a short distance and raised its wings. These motions together with the bird's shaggy appearance, help to identify the species. There is a white phase. 76cm. (30")

Green-backed Heron, *Butorides virescens.* This species often nests in colonies, but it is not restricted to such locations. Almost any small stream or bit of water will attract it. Thus the species is widely scattered, especially in the northern parts of its range. Until recently, it was known as the Green Heron. (The bird illustrated is waiting for food to appear.) 46cm. (18")

Cattle Egret, *Bubulcus ibis.* The Cattle Egret spends much of its time in the presence of cattle, feeding on insects and the like which the animals attract or stir up from the ground. It is not limited to the pastures, however; I have observed it foraging on well-manicured playgrounds, in back yards, and along boulevards. 56cm. (22")

Northern Shrike, *Lanius excubitor.* Birds do not always appear in their natural colors. It looks as though this shrike sat down in something that discolored its outer tail-feathers which normally are white. Northern Shrikes have a rather pleasant and lengthy song on their breeding grounds, in spite of the occasional notes that seem to be out of place. 25cm. (10")

Egret. Several of the birds were busily engaged in picking up insects from the ground and off the backs of cattle. Every so often, they also reached out and quickly captured insects from the air.

Some species display a great deal of intelligence while feeding. During a dry spell sometime ago, I watched a Common Grackle turn over the debris in a rain gutter on my neighbor's garage. It worked systematically from one end to the other. Some species get themselves into awkward situations. One day in late spring, after a light snowfall, I watched a Brown Thrasher trying to break a kernel of corn. Not being equipped with powerful jaws, and being unable to hold the grain with its feet, it was spearing the grain with the point of its bill. It did not simply pick at the grain; it dived upon it, using its wings.

Not everything is harmonious among birds at feeding time. Those people who feed birds regularly know that jays will drive off smaller birds, including the cardinals, and that blackbirds are able to drive off the jays. There is great competition. Something that resembles robbery is when Bald Eagles force the Osprey to give up its fish. They are able to obtain their own prey but apparently they cannot pass by an opportunity to steal it from others.

In contrast to the above, some species become involved in cooperative efforts, although many of them are incidental. In Wisconsin, where the Tundra Swans are common in spring, various species of ducks keep company with them on their feeding waters. They are simply taking advantage of the foods brought to the water's surface by the long-necked swans. Herons may be observed in the vicinity of foraging mergansers, hoping to pick up the small fish they stir up. Cedar Waxwings sometimes line up and pass berries from one bird to another, but I suspect the birds that do the passing are too full to eat another berry.

Occasionally, we hear of misfortunes in connection with the feeding habits of birds. In Wisconsin, my office received a photograph of a Ruffed Grouse with a snake about half swallowed. The grouse could not handle it and died in the attempt. Fish-eating birds sometimes get caught in a similar predicament by attempting to swallow a fish that will not go down. Rattlesnakes give birds a hard time. I recently heard of a hawk that killed a rattlesnake, but died soon thereafter from poisonous bites.

For what length of time can a bird go without food? This question often comes up in connection with their management. It is known that insect eaters cannot endure a long fast. Birds that feed mostly on seeds can hold out longer, particularly the larger species. Weather conditions have a lot to do with this. All things being equal, a Ring-necked Pheasant, for example, can go without food for two weeks or more and still make a comeback.

A few species of birds overeat at times as though they fear a food shortage, but this is unusual. Song birds do not commonly overeat, for they need all the speed and agility they can muster to keep out of reach of their enemies. Excess weight would only be a handicap. Some pelagic species, that obtain most of their food at sea, incubate for long periods at a time and as a result may become emaciated.

Not many birds put away food items for future use. Some species of woodpeckers store nuts quite regularly, though, and certain species of the crow family, including Clark's Nutcracker and the Gray Jay, commonly lay up at least a few things. Any food caches such as these are frequently raided by other species of birds or by

Greater Flamingo, *Phoenicopterus ruber.* One of the unique features of the flamingo is its upside-down bill. The upper mandible, contrary to what we would expect, is hinged, enabling the bird to gather food while holding it upside-down. Further, both mandibles are equipped with *lamellae* (toothlike serrations on each side of the bill), which enable the bird to expel unwanted water while holding on to its food. 114cm. (45″)

Ruddy Turnstone, *Arenaria interpres.* Ruddy Turnstones eat a variety of foods, including both vegetable and animal. The photo shows a turnstone pecking at what is known as a jellyfish. (Actually, this is not a fish, for it has no bones.) In addition, and in accordance with its name, the turnstone finds many things to eat under stones. 23cm. (9″)

Black Skimmer, *Rynchops niger.* In keeping with its name, this is the species that habitually skims the water's surface with its elongated lower mandible. It is a pleasure to watch it in its search for food, for no species is more graceful in flight. Fish and crustaceans of various kinds are included in its diet. 46cm. (18")

Work of the Pileated Woodpecker, *Dryocopus pileatus.* Pileated Woodpeckers visit small wood lots occasionally, but in my experience, they seem to feel the most secure in extensive tracts of mature timber. Here, they find insect food in logs that have fallen to the ground, as well as in standing trees. Carpenter ants, found in the hearts of trees, are a favorite item of food.

mammals, with the result that the owners get very little out of them. However, it also appears that the owners may neglect them or forget where they are located.

What Birds Eat

In adverse weather, some species have difficulty finding food. Not all is lost, however, as many species have alternative methods. In prolonged rainy weather when the air is cleared of flying insects, swallows and swifts pick aquatic insects from the surface of the water. Similarly, flycatchers pick up insects from the ground when necessary.

While looking for birds on a windy day in Alberta, I found Horned Larks and Chestnut-collared Longspurs foraging on the leeward side of long rows of weeds and tall grass. On the same day, Cliff Swallows were picking off insects from the tops of stalks of grain.

Those species that feed heavily on insects, but spend the winters in northern latitudes, are able to find insects in their dormant stage.

The birds of North America eat a great variety of foods. In the vegetable kingdom, seeds, berries, other fruits, nuts, roots (aquatic), leaves, blossoms, buds, twigs, nectar, and sap may be taken. Included among the insects are grasshoppers, crickets, termites, dragon flies, thrips, true bugs, leafhoppers, aphids, beetles, moths, butterflies, wasps, flies, bees and ants. Among the other *Arthropods* taken are spiders, daddy longlegs, crayfish, crabs, and shrimps. Among the *mollusks,* snails, squid, oysters, and clams may be mentioned. Of the reptiles and amphibians consummed are lizards, snakes, salamanders, frogs, and toads. Mammals taken include moles, shrew, bats, mice, rats, squirrels, prairie dogs, and rabbits. Many kinds of fishes and birds are regularly eaten. Grit appears to be very important, not only as an aid in grinding food, but also for its mineral content. Salt is needed by certain species.

Other Ways of Birds

Of all the things that birds can do, flying is the most distinctive. A bird that looks awkward on land is quickly transformed into a spectacular sight when in the air. I shall never forget the flight of forty-three American White Pelicans I saw in Kansas one spring day. What beauty! What adaptability! Perhaps the pelicans were taking advantage of rising warm air currents, called thermals. Gulls and hawks make frequent use of such updrafts. Little effort is required on the part of the birds to sail on these thermals. A simple tilt of the tail, or a slight bend of the wingtip may be all that is required. When a bird flies, the flight feathers of the wing close and overlap on the downstroke, and open, venetian blind style, on the upstroke. Thus a bird can fly upward. The tail also assists in elevating the body.

Some aquatic species such as the coot, use their feet as an aid in becoming airborne. The Mallard, on the other hand, can thrust itself vertically into the air by simply placing its wings flat on the water. When landing on the water, the Mallard skids on its "heels" to help break its momentum.

Some species, such as the goldeneyes, are noisy in flight, but most owls can fly silently or nearly so, because of the fleecy nature of their wings and tail.

How Fast Do Birds Fly?

Sportsmen like to point to the teal as one of the fastest. It can fly 80 kilometers (50 mi.) or more per hour. Falconers boast of the speed of the Peregrine Falcon. It has been timed at about 129 kilometers (80 mi.) per hour, and perhaps can fly even faster than this

Clark's Nutcracker, *Nucifraga columbiana.* The nutcracker, so-named because of its liking for pinyon pine seeds (often called nuts), was discovered by William Clark, of the famed Lewis and Clark Expedition. It has some of the characteristics and ways of woodpeckers, but in structure and behavior, it is very much like our crows. Nutcrackers nest commonly in pines, often near the timber line in our highest mountains. 33 cm. (13")

Golden-crowned Kinglet, *Regulus satrapa* (male) During the winter, Golden-crowned Kinglets travel regularly in small flocks of their own kind, or join with other compatible species. Their *tzee* calls bring them to our attention. We may see them hovering in midair as they search for small insects in the outer branches of a pine or other coniferous tree. 10 cm. (4")

Black-capped Chickadee, *Parus atricapillus.* I have never witnessed a fight among chickadees. Whenever they get together, whether there be one or two, or a flock of six or eight, they always seem to be on friendly terms. The same can be said when housekeeping is taken up in the spring. The pair excavates the nest cavity in a very congenial manner, each individual taking its turn, one after the other. 13 cm. (5″)

Eastern Kingbird, *Tyrannus tyrannus.* In Wisconsin, we commonly see our first Eastern Kingbirds along the roadside fences about the first of May. We are impressed when we see them arrive so punctually, for we realize that they spend the winters in South America. Nesting activities begin shortly after the birds arrive. We find their nests in trees and shrubs, and occasionally on fence posts. 20 cm. (8″)

when necessary. The majority of birds though, average from 40 kilometers (25 mi.) to 48 kilometers (30 mi.) per hour.

How Do Birds Avoid Colliding With One Another When Flying In Flocks?

Shorebirds are good examples of this problem. It seems that they are able to stagger their positions so that one bird is never directly behind another.

The Use Of Feet

Not all birds like to fly. Sportsmen who hunt pheasants regularly know this only too well. The Ring-necked Pheasant prefers to run and hide in a thicket or in a crevice, rather than to fly. It may be able to outrun our native birds, for its speed has been measured at 32 kilometers (20 mi.) per hour.

Robins run for short distances while looking for food. House Sparrows hop along the ground. European Starlings are good walkers. A few species seldom use their feet. These are the strong fliers.

In keeping with these many ways of ground travel, we find that toes, feet, and legs differ in size, shape, and strength. The herons have long legs; the Willow Ptarmigans have feathers on their feet; and the Northern Jacanas have exceptionally long toes. We commonly think of ducks and geese as the birds with webbed toes, but many shorebirds have toes that are partly webbed.

Anyone who has banded hawks knows how a bird's toes can grip; but if the bander holds the feet and legs straight backward, the bird is unable to grip anything. If he allows the bird to bring its feet forward, however, the bander is at the mercy of the hawk, even though he wears leather gloves. Thus we see how a sleeping bird can retain its hold on a circular branch. The tight grip of the toes is automatic while the bird is seated. In order to release the grip, the bird must raise its body. This mechanical arrangement does not interfere with the bird's normal activities. Many species perch in the way described for hawks, but not all species.

The part of the bird's foot immediately above the toes, commonly called the leg, is actually the tarsus. In many species, this part of the foot is scaly.

Birds And Water

That our water birds are excellent swimmrs is axiomatic. That our song birds can swim is not so self-evident. Recently, a young Marsh Wren (formerly Long-billed Marsh Wren) that I was trying to photograph, sat still for a few seconds and then dropped into the water. To my surprise, it swam for a distance of 1.5 meters (5 ft.) before taking a perch on a prostrate rush. This is not to say that song birds can do this *well.* Many fall into the water while migrating, never to rise again.

Some species like to swim entirely submerged. While attempting to photograph a Pied-billed Grebe one day, I noticed to my disappointment that it spent more time under water than above. Further it was able to sink into the water without diving. I was pleased, however, that it stayed within my camera range. The Common Loon, in contrast, often swims a long distance under water before coming to the surface. There are deep divers too. The Oldsquaw is a good example of this, for it has been captured in fishermen's nets at depths of about 53 meters (175 ft.).

While at a zoo one day, I noticed two Mallards pursuing what appeared to be a hybrid. As soon as they captured the off-colored duck, the two Mallards held it under water for a long time as though they wanted to drown it. (I had heard of normal birds doing this to

Pied-billed Grebe, *Podilymbus podiceps.* Because of its wide distribution, this species is our best-known grebe. It can be overlooked, though, as it spends much of its time either under water or within the cover of marsh vegetation. It eats a variety of foods, but as shown in the photograph, it includes fish in its diet. 33cm. (13″)

Hybrid: The pale duck illustrated here appears to be part male Mallard and part white duck of some kind. We may expect to see such hybrids in zoos and in large flocks of tame ducks in the suburbs of cities. We do not expect to find them very often in the wild, although some species of ducks do hybridize occasionally.

Anhinga, *Anhinga anhinga.* Anhingas differ from some of our water birds in that they have to take time out to dry their feathers. The bird shown here was photographed in Florida, where the species may be found nesting virtually year-round. They build their nests in trees such as mangroves and willows, both parents helping with all the work. 89 cm. (35″)

Northern Shoveler, *Anas clypeata.* (male) Perhaps the most conspicuous feature about this species is its bill. Why is it so long and wide? Why does it droop? Actually the bird uses it to plough the water for food. Minute forms of animal life are retained in the bill while the water is strained out through the sides. (The bird shown here is in winter plumage.) 48 cm. (19″)

freaks.) The Mallards held the hybrid under water for about eight minutes, after which the latter escaped. I didn't know it at the time, but I find now that certain deep diving birds can remain under water even longer than ten minutes without harm.

When a scaup dives for a swim under water, it first leaps from the water's surface into the air. The Mallard does not dive for food, but merely tips up to reach a bit of food down in the water. The Brown Pelican dives into the water from a considerable height.

The majority of water birds can shed water easily, but the Anhinga is one of the exceptions. It has to spread its wings in order to dry them.

The Bird's Bill

Bills vary in size, shape and function. The woodpecker is able to chip off wood, the Evening Grosbeck can crack seeds, and the hummingbird extracts nectar from flowers. The American Woodcock is able to probe deeply into the soil for earthworms as the tip of its upper mandible is flexible. Thus we note that the structure of the bill is tied in closely with the feeding habits of the species. The color of the bill may change seasonally in some species, and there may be projections of various kinds on the upper mandible.

Special Use Of Salivary Glands

Chimney Swifts make a special use of the secretions of their salivary glands when they glue their nests to the inner walls of chimneys. A nest I saw freshly made appeared to be varnished.

Not All Birds Have Crops

Owls, for example, have no crop. In doves, the so-called milk for the young is provided by the crop. In most species, the crop, if present, serves primarily as a storage place for food that will be digested later.

Birds And The Weather

Birds have a very rapid heart beat and a temperature in some species as high as 112° Fahrenheit (43° Celsius). Birds do not have sweat glands, but they have other ways to keep cool, one of which is panting with their bills open.

In cold weather, birds fluff out their feathers to insulate themselves. Some species, in addition to this, seek shelter in cavities. While checking deer yards in northern Wisconsin, I occasionally flushed Ruffed Grouse from deep snow. These birds have the habit of plunging themselves into the snow as one way of protecting themselves from the most severe cold. They are comparatively safe from their enemies here too, as they do not leave a trail of tracks.

Some species learn ways of keeping warm. I have often seen European Starlings sitting on the tops of smoking chimneys during cold weather, and I have been told that they sometimes seek shelter in empty tin cans in city dumps. Although most birds can stand the cold temperatures of their normal range, sudden cold or unusual weather does take its toll. Banders tell us that Mourning Doves may have their toes frozen off in severe weather.

Unusual Stress

Birds have certain adaptations to unusual stress. Some species living at high altitudes have larger hearts[2] and lungs[3] than their close relatives of the lowlands, and

[2] R.A. Norris and F.S. Williamson. "Variation in relative heart size of certain passerines with increase in altitude." *Wilson Bulletin,* 67: 78-83. 1955.

[3] W.A. Dunson. "Adaptation of heart and lung weight to high altitude in the robin." *Condor,* 67: 215-219. 1965.

Least Flycatcher, *Empidonax minimus.* It is along the brushy edges of woodlands that we often hear the *che-bec* call of the Least Flycatcher. This call is rendered so phonetically accurate that once it has been heard, it cannot be easily forgotten. The accent is on the second syllable. We may look for the birds in both coniferous and deciduous habitat. 13 cm. (5")

White-breasted Nuthatch, *Sitta carolinensis.* (male) This nuthatch appears to be most at home in deciduous trees. It finds its food here, and it may be that knotholes and other natural cavities are most plentiful in such trees. Families of the birds seem to be closely-knit, and the parents (pairs) are known to remain together in successive years. In winter, pairs are often found to be traveling together. 14 cm. (5.5")

Upland Sandpiper, *Bartramia longicauda.* This sandpiper, known until recently as the Upland Plover, is a bird of the open grasslands, nesting either in the uplands away from water or in lower elevations where water is present. A typical nest is situated on the ground, in a clump of grass. Differing from those shorebirds that normally rest on the ground, Upland Sandpipers commonly perch on fence posts. 30cm. (12″)

Ruddy Duck, *Oxyura jamaicensis.* (male) Ruddy Ducks nest commonly in fresh-water marshes. A peculiarity at this time is that females of this species, and others in the neighborhood such as Cinnamon Teal, Redhead, and Canvasback feel impelled, occasionally, to lay their eggs in one another's nests, especially in those of the present species. 41cm. (16″)

those species that spend most of their time on the wing are likely to have large hearts.

The Feathers of Birds

Anyone who has plucked a chicken knows what a change the operation makes in the appearance of the bird. Birds in their natural attire look as though they are evenly covered with feathers, but in most species the feathers grow in tracts (rows). They grow out of the flesh, but the primary and secondary feathers of the wing are attached to the bones. Feathers do not fall out easily, except during the molting season, and if a few are accidentally lost, they are quickly replaced. Feathers grow from their bases only and have no life in them once they are formed.

Birds normally molt soon after the breeding season. In many species, the feathers are lost and replaced a few at a time, permitting the birds to carry on in a normal way. In ducks and geese, though, the primary feathers drop out all at the same time, disabling the birds for a few weeks. Of course they can still swim during this period. In spring, certain species have a type of molt in which the tips of the feathers wear off, but this is not a handicap. Some species are able to shed a mass of feathers at once, not as a molt, but possibly as a means of defense. When I was banding Mourning Doves, I often ended up with a handful of feathers from each bird.

Body Care

Body care seems to be very important to the birds. Some take a water bath even in cold weather. In addition to water baths, there are sun baths and dust baths. With all of this, there is a lot of feather preening. One kind of preening, not fully understood, has to do with ants. Many species of birds pick up ants and rub them along the surfaces of their feathers.

Color Patterns

Each spring, I get a good look at the Rufous-sided Towhee from my window. It comes to my bird feeder which is located at a low elevation. Thus I get to see the color pattern of its back. Whenever the bird hops forward, it flashes its wings, revealing a small white spot for a second. Each year, when I see this, I am reminded that moving color patterns must be important to birds.

With a few glaring exceptions, birds are paler in color below than above. When the female differs in color from the male, she usually (not always) is the plainest of the two. Further, when the female is plainer than the male, the young usually resemble her. The males, if they have more than one plumage, are at their best during the season of courtship.

Recently, I photographed a young male American Redstart. Except for a small, dark spot on its breast, it looked very much like the adult female. This reminds us that not all birds assume adult plumage during their first year of life, and some do not acquire it for several years. Gulls are especially troublesome to me in this respect. Some birds, such as certain species of grouse, have visible air sacs which may be colorful. The Magnificent Frigatebird has a conspicuous throat sac or pouch.

Unnatural colors sometimes show up on birds. One of the most common of all is white (albinism). I have heard of a number of albinic robins. A second common departure is black (melanism), such as found on the Rough-legged Hawk. Some Eastern Screech-Owls are reddish instead of gray. Years ago, I saw this variation in North Carolina and Virginia, but do not know the extent of their range. I have never seen the reddish phase in

American Redstart, *Setophaga ruticilla.* The first-year male redstart resembles the adult female, except that, as shown here, the breast is somewhat spotted. Also, the plumage that is yellow on the female, is tinted slightly with orange. Occasionally, these young males are able to secure mates. (I took my photograph in May.) 13 cm. (5″)

Eastern Screech-Owl, *Otus asio.* Occasionally, the Screech-Owl may be seen during the day, either at the entrance of its home where it sometimes stands for hours at a time, or on a tree branch where, if frightened, it will compress its plumage and raise its *ears* straight upward. There are two color phases, gray or brown. 23 cm. (9″)

Blue-winged Warbler, *Vermivora pinus.* This warbler has an insectlike song. It consists of two parts, the first of which is the highest in pitch. The second part, in my opinion, is the longest and loudest of the two. Hybrids between this species and the Golden-winged Warbler, called, respectively, Brewster's and Lawrence's, have songs that cannot be readily distinguished from those of the parent species. 13 cm. (5")

Golden-winged Warbler, *Vermivora chrysoptera.* (male) The Golden-winged Warbler may be found in both wet and dry habitat. Often it is found in forest clearings which have grown up to brush. Whether the latter has enabled the species to move northward in the Midwest, I suppose can be debated, but it seems that it has. The species is daintily attired. 13 cm. (5")

the Midwest, although I have observed many Eastern Screech-Owls here. My experiences with the Ruffed Grouse have been similar—reddish phase in the Blue Ridge Mountains and gray phase in the Midwest. This reddish phase is called *erythrism*. When yellow replaces the normal plumage color, this is *xanthockroism*. I have never seen an example of this in the field. Lastly, there are *hybrids* and *mutants*. Perhaps the Brewster's and the Lawrence's warblers are the best-known hybrids among our song birds. They are the progeny of Golden-winged Warblers and Blue-winged Warblers. Mallards sometimes mix with Northern Pintails or other species to produce hybrids; there are others. Mutants occur, occasionally, among birds in laboratory experiments.

Sight And Sound

Does the robin locate its food in the ground by sight or by sound? Some observers believe it is by sight only; others are equally convinced that it is by sound. Both senses (seeing and hearing) are well developed in birds, especially in the nocturnal species.

I have often been impressed by the ability of such species as the Ruby-crowned Kinglet to locate minute objects which constitute much of its food. Many birds look at objects with only one eye. This is especially noticable in hawks when they look upward. Owls use both eyes. They turn their heads almost entirely full circle when necessary to follow an object. When photographing owls, I have been amazed at the way they jerk their heads up and down, or crane their necks forward to get a better focus on the camera.

Taste and Smell

As these two senses are somewhat coordinated, it is difficult to determine to what extent each is functional in birds. Probably their use varies with the species. In my experience, most birds decide quickly whether a given item of food is palatable or not.

Instinct Versus Learning

We commonly say that birds are governed by instinct. When a bird builds a nest for the first time, it produces a model that is recognizable of its species. Precocial chicks recognize the calls of their parents to "freeze," to scurry for cover, or to come out from cover. All species recognize their peculiar enemies. The impulse to do things comes also on a calendar basis, so instinct is tied in with physiological impulses. The instinct of birds is "geared" for the preservation of the individual and of the species.

Although instinct seems to be dominant, birds can also learn. When European Starlings warm themselves atop a chimney in cold weather, they have learned something. When domestic chickens come running at the call of their keeper, they have learned to associate food with a certain sound. When gulls follow a ship, they associate it with food.

How Long Do Birds Live?

Banding records show that pelagic species are among the leaders. A Laysan Albatross has been recorded at forty years. An Arctic Tern survived for longer than thirty-four years, and many gulls appear to be long-lived. As far as smaller birds are concerned, it is seldom that they survive longer than six to eight years. There are exceptions, of course. A White-throated Sparrow is known to have lived for nineteen years, a Black-and-White Warbler for more than eleven years, and a Chimney Swift for a period of ten years.

American White Pelican, *Pelecanus erythrorhynchos.* When I took the picture of the flock, I got the impression that the birds were on their way to their nesting ground in the Northern Great Plains. They commonly nest on islands that are devoid of trees and shrubs. The nestlings have a difficult time here, though, as it takes at least two months for them to learn to fly. 157 cm. (62")

American Crow, *Corvus brachyrhynchos.* One reason why the American Crow gets along so well is its ability to adapt to the situation at hand. The one I photographed was perched on the top of a car in a parking lot. In winter, large flocks take shelter in the suburbs of cities if trees are plentiful. 51 cm. (20")

Crested Caracara, *Polyborus plancus.* The Crested Caracara is peculiar in that it combines some of the characteristics of both hawks and vultures. It is about the size of the Osprey, and resembles it somewhat in profile. It is able to capture its own food, but it often robs other species of their catch, or else resorts to carrion. 56 cm. (22″)

Great Horned Owl, *Bubo virgianus.* This owl is well-named, for both its body and its *horns* (ear tufts) are large in size. When seen from the rear, its head and body appear to be very broad. There are many forms, so colors vary. The bird shown here was photographed in Wisconsin. 58 cm. (23″)

Roosting Habits

One night when returning from a field trip, my companion and I looked out of the car window to see a tremendous roost of Red-winged Blackbirds on a cattail marsh. The night was dark, but the city lights illuminated the marsh. Apparently the birds had learned that the habitat within the city limits was as safe or safer than that without. On another night, I was walking around the capitol square of a city, when I noticed a large flock of House Sparrows roosting in a bare tree. Again the area was well lighted. (This in spite of the fact the House Sparrows are able to build roost nests and often do.)

Not all birds would dare to roost in such exposed places. In fact many species look for the most remote spot they can find. Thus we find robins roosting in cane brakes in the South, Chimney Swifts in chimneys, and bluebirds in tree cavities. Birds, no doubt hope that they will be concealed from their enemies.

Those species that roost in large flocks (crows, eagles) are easily observed as they gather for the night. Certain other species roost as individuals, and these are seldom noticed as they retire. When birds roost, they tuck their bills under their feathers—not under their wings.

Flocking

Certain species have an inclination to flock with others of their kind. Some do not. All stages of flocking exist among North American birds. The Canada Goose likes to keep its family together in addition to staying with its fellows in general; the Purple Martin finds it congenial to nest in flocks as well as to migrate together; the Broad-winged Hawk will migrate in a group, but during the nesting season it prefers to separate; the Cedar Waxwing feeds together as a flock, but during the nesting season it establishes its own territory. Non-breeding birds, such as the first- or second-year gulls, may flock together for a season.

It is interesting to speculate on the advantages and disadvantages of flocking. How does a bird feel when flying in a flock as compared to flying alone? Does it feel more secure if it can roost in flocks? Some birds come together in flocks for incidental reasons. A lack of suitable habitat or the presence of food may serve to congregate a number of species. If the birds are migratory, a sudden change in the weather may temporarily halt a variety of species.

Cycles

Some species are cyclic. They appear to do well for a certain number of years and may increase greatly, only to drop off sharply in numbers within a short period of time. Duration of the cycle may be three to five years, or ten to eleven years, depending upon the species involved. Certain grouse, owls, and hawks are among those species thought to be regularly cyclic. Why some species, and not others, are cyclic is not fully understood.

Range Fluctuations

Considerable interest has been expressed in the range fluctuations of certain species of birds. Why have the Northern Cardinal, the Northern Mockingbird, and the Turkey Vulture, to mention a few, moved northward in recent years? Why have the Brewer's Blackbird, the Western Meadowlark, and the Yellow-headed Blackbird moved eastward? Some observers believe that young birds are prominent among such wanderers, others think that changes in the habitat may be responsible. Perhaps the former environment has deteriorated, or the species needs more room. Changes in vegetation,

Little Blue Heron, *Egretta caerulea.* Little Blue Herons are colonial in nesting habits and usually join other species in forming a large rookery. Their bodies are dark in color (not really blue), but their bills show true blue. The immatures are white, and when making the transition to adult color, appear to be spotted. 61 cm. (24″)

White Ibis, *Eudocimus albus.* Isolated individuals of this species are seldom seen, for the birds feed together, roost together, and nest in colonies. When attempting to photograph an individual (I like to feature only one bird), I had trouble getting it separated from its pals. The long, slender, decurved bill helps to identify the ibises. 63 cm. (25″)

Northern Cardinal, *Cardinalis cardinalis.* (female) The presence of waste grain and weed seeds, I believe, has encouraged the Northern Cardinal to spread northward, and possibly westward in the Mississippi Valley region. Windbreaks and shelterbelts planted by man on the Great Plains may afford nesting sites and winter protection not formerly available to it. 22cm. (8.5″)

Brewer's Blackbird, *Euphagus cyanocephalus.* (male) The name of this species has nothing to do with the manufacture of beer. Audubon named it for Thomas Brewer, a prominent ornithologist of his day. I photographed the bird shown here during the winter. In spring the males acquire a more glossy plumage, especially about the head. The species appears to be moving eastward today. 25cm. (10″)

caused by man, may be involved. Lastly, the species in question, may simply be reclaiming territory which it formerly occupied.

Concluding Remarks

We cannot describe the ways of birds without realizing that there will be exceptions to the rule. As one scientist put it recently, "There are no absolutes in Nature."

Chapter 4

GENERAL CONSERVATION AND BIRDS

"The nation behaves well if it treats the natural resources as assets which it must turn over to the next generation increased, and not impaired in value."
—Theodore Roosevelt

I am using the word "conservation" in the title because it has been associated with the preservation of birds and other wildlife for many years. Today it has a broader use. Many people and governmental agencies think of "conservation" as including just about everything in the environment.

In America much has been accomplished in the field of conservation, especially during the era from about 1930 to the present time. I have found it interesting to keep notes on the history of conservation, particularly as it pertains to birds, so I shall include a few of the highlights of my study in the pages that follow.

Era Of Exploitation

In North America, the nineteenth century was an era of exploitation of our natural resources. Birds of almost any species were hunted freely, and the larger birds, especially, were sold on the market. To add insult to injury, much of the habitat needed by these species was destroyed.

Thankfully, some people were ahead of their times. In 1851, Maine passed a law against the taking of song

Much of the historical information on pages 205 through 216 is gleaned from Don Strode, "History of Wildlife Conservation in the United States," *Alaska Fish Tales and Game Trails,* July-August; September-October, 1972.

Snowy Egret, *Egretta thula.* The Snowy Egret is distinguished by its black bill, dark legs, and yellow feet (toes). Its nuptial plumage is even more elegant than that of the Great Egret, so the species suffered (in early days) the same exploitation at the hands of the plume hunters as the larger egret. Today, however, it is regaining much of its original range. 61 cm. (24″)

Great Egret, *Casmerodius albus.* This picturesque species, formerly called the Common Egret, has been a welcome addition to the avifauna of the upper Midwest, and elsewhere, in recent years. For a long time, it was one of several species overly exploited for its plumes. After the nesting season, it moves northward, sometimes as far as Canada. 96 cm. (38″)

Ring-necked Duck, *Aythya collaris.* We often think of this species as a bird of the open prairie, and so it is, but it nests farther east than our Redhead, for example, thereby indicating that it prefers habitat that is a little more secluded. The species was named for the brownish ring around the neck of the male (often not visible). 43 cm. (17")

Scarlet Ibis, *Eudocimus ruber.* The normal range of this species lies in northern South America, but a few records have been established for it within our boundaries. It is about the size of the White Ibis, and when at rest, it appears to be scarlet throughout, but when in flight, it shows black wingtips. 61 cm. (24")

birds, and during the decade that followed, several additional states followed suit. In 1886, the New York Audubon Society, perceiving the forthcoming doom for our larger birds, tried to have market hunting stopped.

It was a time to start new organizations. In 1883, The American Ornithologists' Union was founded; Theodore Roosevelt, noting that big game was being decimated, started the Boone and Crockett Club in 1887; the Wilson Ornithological Society was founded one year later; and in Massachusetts, a local Audubon Society was started in 1896.

During 1885, C. Hart Merriam, an ornithologist, began work in a branch of the government which later developed into the Bureau of Biological Survey (now the United States Fish and Wildlife Service). Merriam became the first chief of the Bureau and held this position until 1910, when he became research associate of the Smithsonian Institution. After this, H.W. Henshaw and E.W. Nelson had their turns as chief of the United States Biological Survey.

Refuges were started in earnest toward the end of the nineteenth century. In 1870, California established the Lake Merritt Refuge in Oakland; in 1877 Connecticut started the Charles E. Wheeler Refuge on Nell's Island; in 1887 the government established the Last Mountain Lake Refuge in Saskatchewan; and in 1891, Michigan set up refuges on certain marshes bordering the Great Lakes. The now famous Horicon Marsh, in Wisconsin, had its beginning also in 1891.

The majority of these refuges were established primarily for the benefit of ducks and geese as these birds were becoming scarce at the time.

Remedial Legislation

A federal law, known as the Lacey Act, was enacted in 1900. Its purposes were to put an end to the market hunting of both game and nongame species, to stop all importations of so-called harmful birds and mammals, and to prohibit the transportation of illegally gotten game across state borders. It became the cornerstone of all future wildlife legislation.

Members of the Boone and Crockett Club were influential during this period in establishing sound legislation. Theodore Roosevelt, the club's founder, while president of the United States, established the United States Forest Service under Gifford Pinchot and increased the national forests from thirty-three million to one hundred and forty-eight million acres. In 1903, he established the first national bird reservation at the request of The American Ornithologists' Union, on Pelican Island. This was for the benefit of the Brown Pelican in Florida. Since there were no federal wardens in those days, certain members of The American Ornithologists' Union patrolled the island. Roosevelt created fifty-one new national wildlife refuges during 1904.

Although some organizations memorialized the name of John J. Audubon in their official titles, the National Audubon Society was not founded until 1905. The commercialization of egret feathers engaged the attention of this organization at that time, for in 1906 its wardens patrolled three national refuges where colonies of these birds were concentrated. Then in 1908, Audubon wardens patrolled thirty-six additional wildlife refuges, all national, and all containing colonies of egrets or herons.

As the majority of the birds are migratory, a need was felt at this time for a unified national (U.S.)

Brown Pelican, *Pelecanus occidentalis.* Differing from the American White Pelican which moves inland for the summer, this species sticks to the seacoasts throughout the year. It differs also in its manner of feeding, for it dives from the air instead of probing the surface of the water. It has air pockets in the forepart of its body to assist in absorbing the shock received upon striking the surface of the water. 132cm. (52")

Great Blue Heron, *Ardea herodias.* Nesting activities begin during December for this heron, particularly in Florida. Its nest may be built in the tops of trees if the area is wooded; otherwise it may be placed on the ground. In feeding, the birds are not limited to our wetlands, for they include small mammals and land insects in their diet. 119cm. (47")

Steller's Jay, *Cyanocitta stelleri.* This jay is named for Georg Wilhelm Steller, an early day naturalist, who discovered it in Alaska. Its range is far-reaching, but the bird seems to seek out the coniferous forests and avoids the most-barren deserts. It is not migratory in the usual sense, but it does drop down into the lowlands for the winter. 30 cm. (12")

Savannah Sparrow, *Passerculus sandwichensis.* Alexander Wilson originally described the Savannah Sparrow from a specimen collected in Savannah, Georgia. There is no significance attached to the bird's name other than this historical event. Many forms are involved, including some that are virtually nonmigratory, as well as those that are extremely so. (My photograph was taken in the Midwest.) 14 cm. (5.5")

regulatory power. Thus the Weeks-McLean bill was enacted in 1913. This act placed all migratory game birds under federal custody and subject to federal regulations. Then in 1916, the Migratory Birds Conservation Act was formulated, the primary purpose of which was to unify the federal protective laws of Canada and the United States. It was passed by the Canadian Parliament in 1917, and was ratified by the United States Congress in 1918. It effectively ended market shooting, and established the primary authority of the federal governments of both nations to regulate the hunting of migratory game birds, and to take needed steps to assure their preservation. It also provided full protection for many beneficial nongame species. The above treaty did not go far enough, so the United States Migratory Bird Conservation Act was established in 1929. This act authorized, among other things, a system of waterfowl refuges. The treaty between Canada and the United States, as mentioned above, did not include Mexico. However, in 1936, a similar treaty was signed by Mexico and the United States.

A New Approach

As Theodore Roosevelt had played a prominent part in conservation matters during the opening years of the twentieth century, so during the 1920's we find Professor Aldo Leopold entering the scene. Before becoming a professor of wildlife management, Aldo Leopold wrote in the bulletin of the American Game Association to the effect that game is a crop that must be positively managed rather than negatively protected. This was a new approach to wildlife conservation.

In 1928, the American Game Association held a public meeting on conservation matters. This became known as "The First American Game Conference." A committee was formed, with Leopold as chairman, to formulate a national game policy. Later this policy became known as "The American Game Policy." It emphasized the need for the acquisition of scientific facts on game species and for certain changes to come about in the existing conservation departments. The general effect was to take game management out of politics. It further emphasized the need to compensate the landowner for game raised on his land and to foster better cooperation between the sportsman and the landowner. It suggested that men be trained for skillful management positions and fact finding, and wildlife management be recognized as a profession. The policy recognized the need for cooperation among nonhunters, scientists, sportsmen, and landowners in formulating programs and financing them. As far as funding was concerned, it recommended that public funds be raised for wildlife as a whole, that sportsmen finance game interests, and private funds be obtained for education and research.

In 1933, Leopold published his book *Game Management*. It was one of the first books concerned with all wildlife.

Another individual who played a prominent part during this period was Jay N. "Ding" Darling. He followed the suggestion detailed above about private financing of education and research by personally contributing one-third of the first year's costs of this endeavor at Iowa State College. This college was the first to set up a training school for prospective fish and wildlife managers. (In 1936, Darling was able to get Cooperative Wildlife Research Units established in land-grant colleges in nine states.) In 1934 Darling was appointed chief of the United States Biological Survey (now called the United States Fish and Wildlife Service),

American Black Duck, *Anas rubripes.* Because of its similarity in color to the female Mallard, this species is often called the Black Mallard. But there are some notable differences in the habits of the two species. The Black Duck seldom gathers in large flocks, it is wary of man, it often nests in wooded country, and it gathers much of its food in salt-water habitat. 58 cm. (23″)

Lesser Scaup, *Aythya affinis.* (male) The Lesser Scaup does everything well. It makes springboard dives from the water's surface, rises up on the surface of the water as though standing on its feet and flutters its wings but goes nowhere, and when ready to relax, turns over on its side and preens its feathers. 43 cm. (17″)

Ring-billed Gull, *Larus delawarensis.* Although this gull spends its winters along our seacoasts, it is often thought of as a bird of the interior. Ever and again, we see flocks of them following the plow in their search for grubs, worms, and grasshoppers. They are slightly smaller than the Herring Gull, with which they can be confused. 51 cm. (20″)

American Coot, *Fulica americana.* Unlike many water birds, American Coots do much of their feeding on land. Among the items taken are insects, snails, seeds, berries, and leaves of plants. They nest in the cover of marshes, though. Their nesting range covers the greater part of North America; and migration may be noted particularly during the months of April and October. 38 cm. (15″)

and in 1935 became the first president of what is now called the National Wildlife Federation. Today this organization issues one of the most widely distributed magazine on conservation matters in the country. It is also famous for its wildlife stamps. The federation has assisted in keeping politics out of conservation by knitting together sportsmen and sportsmen's clubs throughout the land.

Refuge Matters

Several important waterfowl refuges were established during the 1920's. These include the Upper Mississippi River Refuge, which extends from Wabasha, Minnesota to Rock Island, Illinois. This was the first refuge established on which public hunting was specifically authorized. During 1927, the Horseshoe Lake Refuge was set up in Illinois, and in 1928 the Bear River Migratory Bird Refuge was established on the shores of Great Salt Lake.

In 1934, the United States Migratory Bird Hunting Stamp Act was passed. This stamp, which waterfowl hunters must buy, is commonly called the "duck stamp." The act was established in order to provide money for the refuge program, authorized by the Migratory Bird Conservation Act of 1929. Many refuges were started during the 1930's and succeeding years as a result of the waterfowl stamp.

Federal Aid to States

In 1937, the United States government enacted the Federal Aid in Wildlife Restoration Act. It is commonly called the Pittman-Robertson Act, in memory of the two congressmen who sponsored it. It authorizes federal funds to hire trained wildlife workers, to buy or lease land, and to restore or develop wildlife habitat. This program has been a great help to the conservation of wildlife. It fulfills a major part of the requirements of the American Game Policy. One, of many examples, to illustrate the value of the Pittman-Robertson Act, is the restoration of the Wild Turkey. The source of the funds is an excise tax on sporting arms and ammunition.

A similar law, enacted in 1950 and called the Dingle-Johnson Act (United States), authorizes that funds be raised by means of an excise tax on certain fishing tackle. (This was expanded later.) Both of these acts benefit all kinds of wildlife, including birds, and currently, about eighty million dollars are collected and distributed annually to the states.

More Organizations Formed

The upsurge of interest in wildlife matters during the 1930's resulted in the formation of many organizations, among which the following are of interest: the National Wildlife Federation; the North American Wildlife Foundation, which was involved with the Delta Waterfowl Research Station in Manitoba; and Ducks Unlimited. The latter organization is concerned with the restoration and maintenance of the prairie marshes.

In 1946, the Wildlife Management Institute assumed its present name. It had been active in conservation matters for many years prior to this, but under various names. It has been a motivating force for good, and has influenced the actions of many other conservation organizations. It sponsors the annual North American Wildlife and Natural Resources Conference.

The Nature Conservancy, which is dedicated to the

Much of the historical information on pages 217 through 237 comes from the *Outdoor News Bulletin* of the Wildlife Management Institute, Washington, D.C.

Little Blue Heron, *Egretta caerulea.* Immatures of this species are either entirely white, or mixed white and blue-gray (spotted). They do show the blue (in season) of the bill, however. Contrary to what we would expect, birds in subadult plumage are able to breed. (My photograph was taken in Florida, during March.) 61 cm. (24″)

Roseate Spoonbill, *Ajaia ajaia.* The spoonbill locates its nest in low-growing and rather dense stands of trees or shrubs. The young, two to four in number, are fed by regurgitation at first, and remain in the nest for about seven weeks. Both parents assist with all the work. (The birds illustrated are in immature plumage.) 79 cm. (31″)

Pied-billed Grebe, *Podilymbus podiceps.* I photographed this grebe in late winter, in Florida; so, judging by its plumage, it probably is less than one year old. The winter range of the species lies mainly to the south of the latitude of Iowa, but along our coasts, it may extend as far north as the New England States and British Columbia. 33 cm. (13")

Eared Grebe, *Podiceps nigricollis.* This rather dark species is often compared with the Horned Grebe as both species have golden-yellow head plumes. The present species is named for the latter as they seem to grow out of the region of the ear. I obtained my photograph during the winter season, so the bird is pale, and it lacks the head plumes. 33 cm. (13")

preservation of land on which there are rare plants and wildlife, was incorporated in 1951. To date, more than two million acres have been set aside.

In 1961, an International Migratory Bird Committee was formed; and in 1967, a National Program Planning Committee for Migratory Shore and Upland Game Birds was created by the International Association of Fish and Wildlife Agencies.

The following organizations were started during the 1970's: Western Field Ornithologists, The Pacific Seabird Group, Colonial Waterbird Group, and the International Crane Foundation.

During 1982, the Society of Canadian Ornithologists was founded. Realizing that diligent and systematic studies were needed on the birds of Central America and South America, the Neotropical Ornithological Society was founded in 1983. Then in 1984, the National Fish and Wildlife Foundation was organized, the purpose of which is to encourage donations of real property and other gifts to the United States Fish and Wildlife Service.

National Parks

In 1980, the National Park Service doubled its total acreage by setting aside more than forty-three million acres in Alaska. Mount McKinley National Park (two-million acres) had been established there in 1917, about one year after the Park Service was started in 1916. This acreage, added to the enormous acreage which Canada has set aside as parks or sanctuaries, stands as an important victory to ornithologists as well as to birds. These areas will serve as ecological laboratories in the future, for as a rule, they are preserved in their pristine condition. Not to be forgotten, too, are the state and provincial parks and the smaller local parks and sanctuaries.

Use Of Pesticides

During the 1960's attention was focused upon the mounting problem of pesticides. The detrimental effects were now being felt by people as well as by wildlife. The conclusion was reached that certain pesticides must be banned and alternate means of pest control found. Dr. J.J. Hickey was a leader in expediting this matter.

As far as wildlife was concerned, many species had begun to show danger signs. Thus the United States Endangered Species Preservation Act was enacted in 1966. It specified that the welfare of wildlife and plants must be evaluated on the land before a given development project could be started. Funds to carry out the intent of this act were distributed to the states on a cost-sharing basis. A list of endangered species has been drawn up.

In Canada, a federal government policy statement (1966) pledged every effort to prevent the extinction of any wildlife species.

During the late 1970's, the public throughout North America was made aware that pollution in general was becoming a threat in all areas of our environment—air, water, and land.

Nongame Species Given Attention

In 1975, a symposium on the management of forest and range habitats for nongame birds was held in Tucson, Arizona. This was something new and a great step forward. It pointed up some of the skills we must acquire in order to manage nongame birds. Interestingly, in 1976, a law was enacted to insure, among other things, consideration of wildlife in our national forests. It is called the "National Forest Management Act."

As a result of the Tucson symposium four regional workshops on the management of nongame birds were

Hermit Thrush, *Catharus guttatus.* The Hermit Thrush has such an extensive winter range that many people know it well, although they have never seen it in its breeding range nor heard it sing. It is a very successful species, nesting either in a tree or on the ground, depending upon the conditions; and the habitat chosen may be either coniferous or deciduous. 18 cm. (7″)

Swainson's Thrush, *Catharus ustulatus.* The song of this species resembles that of the Hermit Thrush, but in form, it normally ascends the scale. It can be heard regularly during migration, which is usually not the case with the Hermit Thrush. In common with the latter, the bird will give the observer a merry chase through the brush (thorns and all) when a close-up look is desired. 18 cm. (7″)

Red-bellied Woodpecker,
Melanerpes carolinus.
(male) In this species, the back, as well as the wings, are barred, giving rise to such names as *ladder-back* and *zebra-back.* Actually, these names are more fitting than *red-belly,* for the latter mark can be found only on the male, and even here, it is scant. Its calls are distinctive. 24 cm. (9.5″)

Downy Woodpecker,
Picoides pubescens. (female) The range, year-round, covers most of the forested regions of North America, north of Mexico, but the birds do not utilize the deep forests to the same extent as do the Hairy Woodpeckers. Several forms are involved, so there is some geographical variation in color, but this does not create a problem. The species regularly nests in deciduous trees. 16 cm. (6.5″)

held between 1977 and 1980. These were sponsored by the Forest Service of the United States Department of Agriculture and the National Nongame Bird Steering Committee. The fourth workshop considered grasslands in addition to forests.

In 1980, a law was passed authorizing the United States Fish and Wildlife Service to apportion twenty million dollars over a period of four years to the state fish and wildlife agencies for nongame conservation purposes. *All* species of fish and wildlife are included, whether or not they are taken for recreational or economic purposes. The law is called the "Fish and Wildlife Conservation Act."

By the end of 1983, thirty-one states had provided a *nongame wildlife checkoff* on their tax forms, meaning that tax refunds could be turned over directly to the respective fish and wildlife agencies instead of to the taxpayer. Colorado was the first state to adopt this system. The program has been a great success, and the money collected in this way is added to that received from the federal government.

Habitat and the Birds

During the past forty to fifty years, considerable attention has been devoted to land and its use. Not all of this has been favorable to the birds. I shall list below, in chronological order, a few of the transactions that had an effect on the birds.

Much habitat was lost during the 1940's and 50's when a federal agricultural program, designed to encourage the drainage of potholes in the prairie states, was put in effect.

In 1948, the Lea Act was enacted, purposing to alleviate damage to rice and other crops in California and to disperse large concentrations of wintering waterfowl. It authorized the purchase of land on which crops could be grown especially for waterfowl. The hope was to spare crop loss on private land. Hunting on the lands was permitted at the discretion of the Secretary of the Interior. Accordingly, areas in Colusa, Sutter, and Merced Counties, and Salton Sea in California were purchased.

Damage done by the draining of potholes was partly offset during the 1950's when the U.S. Department of Agriculture started the federal land retirement program. In order to help stabilize prices and supplies, farmers were paid to refrain from raising certain crops. As a result, vast amounts of land were allowed to lie fallow. Obviously, this was a help to wildlife.

As of 1962, the Refuge Recreational Act (U.S.) allows public uses of national wildlife refuges that are not detrimental to the original purpose. Examples would be fishing, Nature trails, visitor centers, picnic areas, and certain kinds of hunting.

In 1966, the National Wildlife Area Program was begun by the Canadian Wildlife Service to preserve and manage important or unique lands for wildlife. Originally it was restricted to habitats for migratory birds, but now it includes land for other wildlife.

The United States Water Bank Program, started in 1970, was revised in 1979 to provide thirty million dollars (an increase of twenty million). Its purpose is to offer private landowners annual payments for preserving and protecting important wetlands and adjacent wildlife cover. Since enactment, this program has put nearly six hundred thousand acres of wetlands and adjacent land under protective management for wildlife.

In 1972, Arkansas started a program called "Acres for Wildlife." It has been very successful. Landowners who sign up for it adjust their agricultural practices to benefit wildlife.

Northern Cardinal, *Cardinalis cardinalis.* (male) From the viewpoint of man, the Northern Cardinal is a model species. It sings beautifully, presents an elegant appearance, often comes with its mate to our back yards and bird feeders, nests in our ornamental plantings, and feeds on insects and waste grain. Cardinals are not migratory in the usual sense, but they do move about for food. 22cm. (8.5″)

Purple Finch, *Carpodacus purpureus.* When the Purple Finch was named, the reference was to the royal purple of kings, which was actually red. Thus the adult males are largely red in color, although the upper back, wings, and tail are dark. The bird on the right may be a female, but the immature males are colored in about the same way. 15cm. (6″)

Common Yellowthroat, *Geothlypis trichas.* (male) Many forms of this warbler have been described, but the Common Yellowthroat is the most widespread. It ranges throughout most of North America, except in the more inhospitable parts. There is some geographical variation in color, particularly on the belly (yellow or white); and variations may be noted in the songs. (My photograph was taken in Wisconsin.) 13 cm. (5″)

Chestnut-sided Warbler, *Dendroica pensylvanica.* (male) The Chestnut-sided Warbler spends much of its time in the lower branches of deciduous trees where it can be easily observed. In quality and form, its songs remind us of those of the Yellow Warbler. In a typical song, the accent is on the note next to the last. 13 cm. (5″)

The Canada Wildlife Act of 1973 gave the federal government authority to acquire and manage habitats for migratory birds and, in agreement with provinces or territories, for other species of wildlife.

The United States Bureau of Land Management has under its supervision more than four hundred and fifty million acres of public land. Until recently, rules were vague regarding the management of these lands, so in 1976, the Federal Land Policy and Management Act was signed into law. The first wilderness area to be managed by the Bureau of Land Management was Bear Trap Canyon in southwestern Montana. Arrangements for this were made during 1984.

In 1980, the Great Plains Conservation Program was extended to 1991. Its purpose is to share costs with those landowners who enhance fish and wildlife habitat.

Also during 1980, the United States Congress reauthorized the Coastal Zone Management Act, which provides assistance to states for developing and implementing management programs that protect coastal areas while permitting necessary development. It also added a "coal impact" amendment so that states can ameliorate damage by coal development.

Canada currently has nearly one hundred sanctuaries set up primarily for the welfare of migratory birds.

During 1980, the United States Congress added two large national wildlife refuges in Louisiana. (Total acreage is more than ninety thousand.) They are called respectively, Bogue Chitto and Tensas River. In Alabama, the island of Bon Secour (ten thousand acres) was added to the system.

The Alaska lands bill of 1980 established fifteen refuges (more than fifty-three million acres) in Alaska and added more than fifty-six million acres to its National Wilderness Preservation System and thirteen rivers to its National Wild and Scenic Rivers System.

In Idaho (1980), one hundred and twenty-five miles of the Salmon River was added to the Wild and Scenic Rivers System.

During 1981, the Dow Chemical Company donated forty thousand acres of forested wetlands in the Atchafalaya Basin to the State of Louisiana as part of a preservation program. At about the same time, the Pennzoil Company donated one hundred thousand acres of the Vermejo Ranch in northern New Mexico to the United States Forest Service. This area has many lakes and streams.

As of 1982, Canada is protecting nearly twenty-four million acres of wetlands under the Convention on Wetlands of International Importance. Legislation to protect undeveloped barrier islands along the Atlantic and Gulf coasts from unwise development was enacted in the same year by the United States. It is called the Coastal Barrier Resources Act.

The Nature Conservancy recently turned over more than eleven thousand acres of desert wetland, situated on the California-Nevada border, to the National Wildlife Refuge System. The area is called Ash Meadows Refuge.

During 1984, the Prudential Insurance Company donated one hundred and twenty thousand acres of wetland and forest land to the National Wildlife Refuge System. It is situated along the coast of North Carolina. The Barnegat Bay National Wildlife Refuge, in New Jersey, was enlarged by a gift from AT&T, amounting to two thousand, four hundred acres. A few states set up programs under which landowners could be paid for setting aside a certain amount of cropland for wildlife. Perhaps this program will spread to other states. Near the end of 1984, the United States Army Corps of

Golden-winged Warbler, *Vermivora chrysoptera.* (female) This warbler builds its nest on or near the ground, often in weeds, and in open or semi-open habitat such as brush-covered forest clearings. The nesting range lies to the south of a line drawn from southern Quebec to southern Manitoba, and north of the latitude of southern Ohio; plus the Appalachian Mountains in their entirety. 13cm. (5″)

American Goldfinch, *Carduelis tristis.* (male) Goldfinches are a favorite among naturalists because they seem to embody the very epitome of cheerfulness. Whether they are heard singing alone or in flocks, on a perch or in undulating flight, they always seem to be happy. Their *per-chick-o-ree* flight call serves to identify them, and this may be heard throughout most of the summer. 13cm. (5″)

Sedge Wren, *Cistothorus platensis.* The Sedge Wren occupies the niche between the wet marsh and the dry upland. It suspends its nests (globular in shape) from sedges, forbes, or hay (if the latter has been planted in the lowlands). Often these nests are built near the ground, but the progressive growth of the vegetation to which they are attached may elevate them considerably. 11 cm. (4.5″)

Dark-eyed Junco, *Junco hyemalis.* (female) Juncos nest commonly on the ground, but usually with some overhead protection. We think of them often as birds of the forest edge, but large populations nest in the arctic regions where there are only stunted trees. Several geographical forms have been combined recently. (The female, shown here, was photographed in Wisconsin.) 15 cm. (6″)

Engineers ruled that permits would have to be obtained from them before attempting to dredge or fill in aquatic areas.

Then in 1985, the United States Fish and Wildlife Coordination Act was changed so that federal development agencies, such as the Army Corps of Engineers, must consult with the United States Fish and Wildlife Service to assess habitat damage which may be caused by water projects and other activities. Also in 1985, the United States Fish and Wildlife Service added Buenos Aires Ranch, near Tucson, Arizona, to the National Wildlife Refuge system, for the benefit of the endangered Masked Bobwhite (a form of the Northern Bobwhite). In 1986, the United States National Marine Fisheries Service and the Army Corps of Engineers started a three-year pilot program to create habitat for fish. This, in most cases, probably will help other wildlife, including birds.

As a result of action by the World Wildlife Fund, the states of Delaware and New Jersey established (during 1985) an area where shorebirds could be given special protection. It is known as the Sister Reserves as it includes the lower twenty-five miles of shoreline of Delaware Bay in both states. These reserves, as a unit, represent the second largest shorebird staging area east of the Rocky Mountains. The largest is the Cheyenne Bottoms of Kansas.

Centers of Education

We previously pointed out the value of public lands, such as parks, as centers of education, especially when they are kept in pristine condition. Another activity of special interest to ornithologists is the Canadian Wildlife Service Interpretation Program, now being expanded, and which, eventually, will cover all the major life zones of the Dominion. Interpretation centers are currently situated in, or near, the following locations: Perce, Quebec; Creston, British Columbia; Midland, Ontario; Swift Current, Saskatchewan; and Quebec City on the St. Lawrence River.

First State Law Against Acid Rain

New York was the first state to enact a law against acid rain. In 1984, it passed this law in an effort to reduce sulfur dioxide and nitrogen oxide emissions from oil- and coal-burning power plants and industries.

Governmental Agencies Take Lead

Governmental agencies now regulate all matters pertaining to hunting and the enforcement of conservation laws. They also collect all fees and monies pertaining to hunting and spend them to enhance the same. They purchase, develop, and maintain lands for nesting purposes, for refuges, and for hunting purposes. Since they must manage birds, they study their disease and parasite problems, monitor the population trends of many species, and conduct research to learn new facts. They must check all imports, including what the pet stores can sell, and things pertaining to the welfare of the outdoor environment, including the use of pesticides and herbicides. This includes attention to nongame species. They issue permits to persons who are qualified to possess or raise protected species and have the unpleasant task of issuing control permits when protected species are found to be doing excessive damage.

The above are only some of the things handled by governmental agencies. I have emphasized the functions that have to do with birds.

I said that governmental agencies have the unpleasant task of controlling certain detrimental species. Around airports, for example, it is impossible to fly an

Spotted Sandpiper, *Actitis macularia.* We normally identify this sandpiper by its spotted breast. In the fall, however, there are no spots. Then, its method of teetering, its tendency to fly low over the water, and its shallow wingbeat, help to identify it. The birds do not occur often in flocks, but they are widespread in our land, utilizing open habitat away from water as well as near it. 18cm. (7″)

Semipalmated Sandpiper, *Calidris pusilla.* This sandpiper is thought of primarily as a migrant. It nests in the arctic regions and winters well into South America. It is fairly common, so most observers have seen it. The name directs our attention to the bird's toes which are partly webbed. Actually, the birds can swim real well. 15cm. (6″)

Brown Thrasher, *Toxostoma rufum.* The habitat of the Brown Thrasher falls somewhere between that of the Grey Catbird which may be near water, and that of the Mockingbird, which is frequently near human habitation. The nest is built often in dense shrubbery along roadsides or on the ground where some shelter is available. Usually there will be a tall tree nearby from which the male can sing. 28cm. (11″)

Marsh Wren, *Cistothorus palustris.* Historically, appraisals made of the song of this species have not been glowing, but recently, while photographing near the nest of one, I was impressed by the quality of the closing notes of its usual song. This part of the song, when rendered as the bird flies toward its nest, calls to mind the flight song of the better-known House Wren. 13cm. (5″)

airplane if there are flocks of birds in the way. If a farmer loses a large part of his annual crops because of the depredations of birds, he is entitled to a method of control. Thus public hunting of the species involved in damage is often looked upon with favor. Such hunting not only helps to avoid crop losses, it also brings in some income through the sale of hunting licenses and through certain excise taxes on sporting guns and ammunition. Incidentally, it has been proved that almost *any* species can be managed like an annual crop that can be harvested. Once the momentum has been established, the species will maintain it. Success depends upon the amount of skill that the wildlife manager possesses.

If a person is dissatisfied with existing conservation programs, or wishes to introduce new ones, he has the right to lobby for a policy change, either as an individual or as a representative of an organization. I take it for granted that those who bring forward suggestions for changes will inform themselves beforehand on *both* sides of the question, for in the past, in my experience, much time, effort, and expense has been lost because the suggestions were not well thought out. Is the proposed change practical? Will it do what is expected of it? Will there be repercussions? These are some of the questions that come to mind. Those proposals that include a method of financing the program, usually have the best chance of winning support.

Concluding Remarks

The history of conservation in North America is voluminous. In the above summary, I have not intentionally omitted the names of prominent conservationists—there were hundreds of them. Neither are my explanations of the laws complete. I have simply tried to convey to the newcomer a "feel" for the issues encountered and some of the legislation that resulted. Not all facts and dates of laws are perfectly reliable for not all historians are in agreement, but the above is reasonably accurate. Laws are subject to frequent change.

Blackpoll Warbler, *Dendroica striata.* (male) This warbler has an interesting song. It sounds like the ticking of a large watch. All notes are on the same pitch, but the mid-portion of the song is the loudest. A typical song may consist of six to twelve or more notes. In quality, it is soothing, as it harmonizes with the tranquility of the forest where it is heard. 14 cm. (5.5″)

Connecticut Warbler, *Oporornis agilis.* (male) In common with other ground warblers, the Connecticut Warbler keeps out of sight much of the time. Its song is the thing that brings the bird to our attention. In form, it resembles that of the Ovenbird, but it does not build up in volume toward the end. Wilson named the species for the state of Connecticut as he discovered his first specimen there. 14 cm. (5.5″)

Lesser Yellowlegs, *Tringa flavipes.* This small edition of the Greater Yellowlegs is midway in size between that species and the Stilt Sandpiper. Its usual call, a sort of *yodel,* is normally shorter and softer than the corresponding call of the Greater Yellowlegs. I obtained my photograph in Florida, but the species may be observed throughout the greater part of North America. 25 cm. (10")

Ruddy Turnstone, *Arenaria interpres.* The Ruddy Turnstone is one of our most bizarrely-colored shorebirds, especially when in flight. I took my photograph during April, before the summer plumage was fully developed. The Ruddy Turnstone, a circumpolar species, breeds in the arctic tundra, but a large population migrates through North America to winter in our subtropical regions. 23 cm. (9")

Chapter 5

BIRD RESEARCH

Kirtland's Warbler is currently in the news. As a result of considerable research, it seems that this species requires stands of young pine for its nesting habitat. Thus efforts are made to provide this habitat, on a sustained basis, on the small acreage in Michigan that constitutes its summer range. However, presently, in spite of this help, it seems that the birds are on the decline.

As the species is rare and possibly on the verge of extinction, research continues, but as of this writing, authorities are not agreed as to what to do next. Some believe that the Brown-headed Cowbird may be a major factor in the decline. This could be true as the cowbird is, in my opinion, more abundant in the Midwest today than it was formerly. If it should turn out that the cowbird is the *critical factor* and its numbers can be controlled on the breeding grounds of this warbler, we would have hope for success.

Other authorities believe that the trouble may be in the winter quarters. In any event, we can see the value of research from this experiment, and the need to discover the critical factors involved. Research continues.

How Is Research Conducted?

Bird research is conducted by both professional and nonprofessional workers. The former have learned their methods in college and are well prepared to conduct research, however, the latter may, or may not be well prepared, so I hope that my discussion on the subject will be useful to them.

When a species has been selected as the subject of

research, it is expedient to find out what has been done on it in the past, both in this country and abroad. Information in the latter case may, if necessary, be on closely related species. If work is being done currently by researchers at a distant point, frequent interchange of ideas will be helpful.

As the researcher does not know in advance what will be useful, he must study the entire life history, yearlong, for the species involved. Notes must be taken on all details, both positive and negative. A phenological calendar should be developed for the study area or areas. Events of both the animal and plant kingdom should be recorded as they may have a bearing on the success or failure of the subject species. It is best to work on this in the heart of the species' range, for obvious reasons. Later, research on the fringes of the range may be desirable to round out the picture. An optical device, called the "stratiscope," may be used to make a rapid appraisal of the habitat. It measures the amount of cover, both horizontally and vertically.

After several years of study, when the habitat (food and cover) requirements of the species are known, it may be desirable to alter the habitat of one of the study areas, in various ways or at various times, to note the effect. Ways to help a species may be found in this way.

Usually birds will be marked in some way so that an individual can be followed, as such information is often more meaningful than data on the species as a whole. Marking (under permit) can be done in various ways. On the nesting area, for example, it may be desirable to use leg bands of various colors to serve this purpose, or to paint a few body feathers a special color. Special equipment is now available which will enable the researcher to monitor activities at the nest, without being there, and individual birds can be tracked by

Brown-headed Cowbird, *Molothrus ater.* (male) During the nonbreeding season, cowbirds often mix with other blackbirds, but they are easily distinguished as they are comparatively small in size, and when on the ground, they usually cock their tails at a rather high angle. They have profited by changes wrought by man in their habitat. Cattle now outnumber the bison that formerly were their companions. 19 cm. (7.5")

Brown-headed Cowbird. *Molothrus ater.* (female) The female cowbird, shown here, does not build a nest. She lays her eggs in the nest of another species, usually one smaller than herself. It seems that the female may lay fifteen or more eggs per season (May to July, primarily) in a home territory. Further, the same female may return annually to the same territory, and surprisingly, she may be accompanied by the same male. 19cm. (7.5")

Cattle Egret, *Bubulcus ibis.* The Cattle Egret, a foreign species, has worked its way into North America, apparently on its own power. At this writing, it has reached (in summer) most sections of the lower United States, southeastern Alaska, and many parts of Canada. Apparently it came to us from Africa, by way of South America and the West Indies. 56cm. (22")

European Starling, *Sturnus vulgaris.* Starlings are ever ready to eat. Only a few days ago, I split some oak firewood in my back yard. During the process, many hibernating insects fell to the ground. I picked up my firewood, and upon looking back, saw several starlings eagerly snatching up those insects. How did they know where to come so quickly? 20cm. (8")

means of radio.

In addition to the above work on the nesting grounds, it is desirable to trace the birds during the nonbreeding season. This can be done by means of the standard aluminum bands as furnished by the federal agencies. Longevity, where the birds spend the winter, which migration routes they use, and whether they have homing ability are some of the things that can be learned through this means. Further, with birds in hand, the sex and age usually can be determined. Methods of aging differ with the species, but the bones of the skull do not harden until the bird is of a certain age, and the tips of the feathers of the young of many species remain pointed or notched for a period of time. Moreover, the trapping and marking of birds within their nesting territories may reveal a higher count than the researcher thought possible.

In this activity, as in many others, not all is fun. If the researcher bands the nestlings before they are ready to leave the nest, they may jump out prematurely (sometimes at the urging of the parents) and be captured by their enemies. If the researcher waits until they are ready to leave, he may miss his opportunity. Certain species like to remain together as family groups. Will disturbances such as banding serve to separate them?

Today there are ways to temporarily stupify birds for study purposes, and ways to test them for pesticide residues without killing them. Sometimes it is necessary to kill birds (under permit) for a check of their physiology or for food habits. However, there are now ways to cause a bird to regurgitate food recently eaten without injury to the bird. Pesticide residues that show up in the feathers of birds can be tested and may indicate where the bird originated.

Some researchers like to "imprint" young birds onto

themselves as though they were the parents. This has to be done at a very early age if it is to be successful.

To obtain accurate information on incubation periods, it is necessary to mark the eggs. The number of days required for the last egg laid to hatch is the most accurate.

Sometimes researchers send out questionnaires to certain groups of the public. When this is done, the questionnaire should be kept simple and rather brief for best results. It is of more value to get back replies from a large number of people than from those few who can take the time to wade through a maze of questions.

To terminate a research project is difficult for it seems that there is always something more to be learned. And yet, if the research is to be of value, it must be summarized and turned over to wildlife managers. This applies especially when rare species are being studied.

How Is Research Financed?

Bird research is financed in various ways. Historically, more money has been available for research on game species than on nongame. In the United States, funds have been collected through the sale of hunting licenses, and through a federal excise tax program authorized by the Pittman-Robertson Act of 1937 which provides that a tax must be levied on the sale of sporting guns and ammunition. Today the Fish and Wildlife Conservation Act of 1980 (U.S.) provides funds for nongame species, including birds. Many states are now finding ways to finance nongame programs. Aside from public financing, money in small amounts is occasionally made available for bird research by hobby organizations and by private individuals. Not to be overlooked too, is money, sometimes in liberal amounts, spent by ornitho-

Black-and-white Warbler, *Mniotilta varia* (male) This is the *zebra* among birds. No matter which way he turns, he shows his stripes. He is able to find his food among the smaller branches of trees and shrubs, as many warblers do, but he prefers to creep over the bark of the larger branches and trunks of trees. He is an early spring migrant. 13 cm. (5")

Northern Waterthrush, *Seiurus noveboracensis.* This warbler was named *waterthrush* many years ago because it resembles a thrush in color pattern, and is inclined to live in wet surroundings. It builds its nest on the ground, often under the shelter of upturned tree roots or similar cover, and in moss-covered tree stumps. It has the peculiar habit of teetering its body in sandpiper-fashion. 15 cm. (6")

American Kestrel, *Falco sparverius.* (male) The American Kestrel is one species that may be easily observed along our highways, for it habitually sits on utility wires and poles, or on bare trees. From such points of vantage, it spies its food, although it frequently hovers in midair above fields, apparently for the same purpose. 25 cm. (10″)

Black Vulture, *Coragyps atratus.* This species is slightly smaller than the Turkey Vulture, but in several ways, it is more aggressive. It is more likely to take live animals, and when feeding with the other species, it will be the last to leave if danger threatens. Perhaps it gains some courage in numbers, for in my experience, it often travels in loose flocks. 63 cm. (25″)

logists who like to study birds on their own.

This reminds us that while research of a general nature is useful, research designed to solve specific problems is to be encouraged. Herbert Stoddard, the quail specialist, was one of the first persons to conduct research with better management in view. Today we know quite well how to manage many of our game birds as a result of practical research. No doubt we will continue to make progress.

Research has been started on our nongame species, now that money has been made available for it, but as with the study of game species, answers to management problems come slowly. The same can be said for implementing management programs once they have been prescribed.

Why Is Research Slow?

In a nutshell, research is slow because it is difficult. There are many pitfalls into which the researcher can fall, and these slow down the work considerably. I shall enumerate some of the problems that I have noticed with the hope that they can be avoided by others. As the saying goes—"to be forewarned is to be forearmed."

The basic trouble a species is encountering may be in the tropics, if the species is migratory and winters there. What appears to be the solution to a problem on one acreage may not work at all on another acreage if the surroundings are different. Likewise, birds in a shrinking population may not behave in a way typical of the species.

Predators are attracted by the pandemonium that usually ensues when nests are approached or examined, and mammals may follow in the tracks of man, unless they can be repelled. In many species wherein both sexes attend the nest, one member of the pair is likely to be more diligent than the other. Is this in any way influenced by the presence of the researcher? If the adults are color marked, will they desert one-another because of the change in appearance?

Recently I watched several Cedar Waxwings bathe peacefully in one of my birds baths (shallow water) while in another bath of the same size (deep water), a number of the same species were fighting for positions because only a few could find space in the shallow portions. Had I observed only the latter, I would have concluded that Cedar Waxwings are very belligerent while bathing. Therefore, in research, more than one experiment may be required before making an accurate appraisal.

Certain species may desert their nests if disturbed; with some, it depends upon when the disturbance occurs. When brood counts are made of precocial chicks, some broods observed may be fragmented while others are composed of two or more broods. There may be a saturation point in a given population or combination of populations, and this may vary with habitat conditions as well as geographically. The species under study may be cyclic. Plant succession may drive the species under study to another location. Weather vagaries from year to year may preclude accurate appraisals of nest locations and losses. Finally a study project can be set up in the wrong way or place to begin with.

Qualifications of the Researcher

From the above discussion, it is clear the researcher must have an abiding interest in the subject, an insatiable appetite for knowledge, a desire to save the birds for future generations, an acuity to discern the motives behind the actions of birds (not always the

Osprey, *Pandion haliaetus.* Ospreys are well adapted to their mode of living, their plumage being water-repellent, and their feet arranged so that two toes can be held in front and two behind. They dive into the water, feet first, in order to catch their fish, and when they fly away, they hold the fish head-first instead of crosswise in their claws. 58cm. (23")

White Ibis, *Eudocimus albus.* The bird shown here is an immature White Ibis. I photographed it during the spring, so I suspect that it was at least one year old. (The species does not change color rapidly.) In size, it is similar to the Glossy Ibis. White Ibises eat such things as frogs, crawfish, and insects. 63cm. (25")

White-crowned Sparrow, *Zonotrichia leucophrys.* I have observed White-crowned Sparrows in many parts of North America, but the ones that nest high in the Rocky Mountains impress me the most. There is very little vegetation here—snow and ice persists—and yet the birds sing as though they were in the best possible life zone. I can see from this why they like the tundra and taiga of our arctic regions. 18cm. (7″)

Indigo Bunting, *Passerina cyanea.* (male) As shown here, young males may be spotted or tinged with rusty-brown when they first arrive in their breeding range. (This photograph was taken in May.) 14cm. (5.5″)

same as in human beings), patience and honesty. Fortunately, many workers possess such qualifications and they are capable of discovering the critical factor (or factors) which are required in order to take remedial action. To speed up the work, one researcher may be able to work on more than one species at a time.

Chapter 6

HABITAT MANAGEMENT

During the past fifteen years, I have been watching the creation and development of a certain marsh in Wisconsin. Prior to this undertaking, there were no Yellow-headed Blackbirds nesting in this vicinity. Today, there is a flourishing colony, for the cattails and rushes have grown to full size and the water depth is maintained at the proper level. This has shown me that man can develop good habitat if he goes about it according to a plan.

Habitat Management in General

The subject is not new, but we must intensify our efforts to manage habitat, partly to help certain species of wildlife that are becoming rare, and partly to preserve pristine habitat that is in short supply. Examples of rare birds currently being helped by habitat management are Kirtland's Warbler and the Greater Prairie-Chicken.

One of the major reasons for preserving pristine habitat is to have a natural vegetative pattern to follow when restoring or developing habitat nearby. To preserve pristine habitat and to look after the needs of our rare species are matters of high priority today, but we are not neglecting the more commonplace types of habitat management. Wetlands have been developed where none existed before, trees and shrubs have been planted, and prairie habitat has been maintained. Not to be overlooked too, are the projects wherein land has been set aside to serve *as it is.* The mere fact that it has been set aside is a form of habitat management. Conversely, because of natural plant succession, occasional changes have to be made in projects of long

Yellow-headed Blackbird, *Xanthocephalus xanthocephalus.* (male) This photograph illustrates a marsh that was created in an area where none existed before, and where there were no Yellow-headed Blackbirds. These birds are more particular about where they nest than their neighbors, the Red-winged Blackbirds. They use the cattails, tules, or similar growth, but the water must be deep throughout the nesting season. 25 cm. (10″)

Purple Martin, *Progne subis.* In the mountains of the West, Purple Martins have a strong proclivity to nest in woodpecker cavities and in knotholes of trees, but elsewhere, they seem to prefer bird houses. Such houses are usually built with many rooms as the species is colonial in nesting habits; and they are placed in the open as the birds need space in which to fly. 20 cm. (8″)

Northern Oriole, *Icterus galbula.* (female) As can be seen in the illustration, the female (Baltimore) oriole is more plain in color than the male. This is to be expected as she builds the nest and incubates the eggs, but the male violates this principle as he helps to feed the young. Very little effort is made to conceal the nest. 19 cm. (7.5")

Dickcissel, *Spiza americana.* (male) The Dickcissel, a bird of the alfalfa fields, calls out its name often from high points such as utility wires. In my experience, most people laugh when they hear the song for the first time, not only at the song itself, but also at the bird for being so obliging as to repeat both of its names, *Dick-dick-Cissel-cissel-cissel.* 16 cm. (6.5")

standing if certain species of birds are to be retained. A similar situation prevails among our wetlands. After a certain number of years they (including lakes) fill in and, in some cases, dry up completely. So the management of habitat may take on various forms, depending upon the needs of the locality.

Urban Habitat

As we travel we see many instances wherein city and village agencies have planted trees and shrubs for the benefit of birds. Some have even posted their boundaries to indicate that the entire municipality is a bird refuge.

In any city many of the plants used as ornamentals serve also as food and cover for birds, and this is especially true in desert country. To improve a city, the median strips of boulevards often can be planted with crab apple trees and other food-bearing plants; and city parks, if they are large enough, can be made very attractive to birds when a *variety* of trees and shrubs are planted. We stress variety, as outbreaks of disease may be better discouraged in this way. If the city or village has a stream running through it, or a pond, the opportunities to develop a bird refuge are much enhanced.

In addition to plantings, another project that beautifies a village or the suburbs of a city is the erection of martin houses. Many municipalities develop school forests, and these are valuable from the standpoint of education. When the city parks are of large size, nature trails can be established as an educational feature.

All municipalities should discourage the buildup of large flocks of such exotics as European Starlings and House Sparrows. They are not native here and they do cause a lot of trouble. The buildup of large flocks of

Mallards in cities also can become a problem, for such birds usually do not receive a proper diet. (The development and management of bird habitat on private urban property is discussed in Chapter One.)

Highway Habitat

While traveling through Nebraska several years ago during the nesting season, I noticed that Dickcissels sang at virtually all the cloverleaf intersections of the larger highways. The grass and other vegetation had been allowed to grow fairly tall here, in contrast to the neighboring farm lands. I was convinced then, that our highway right-of-ways can be utilized as bird habitat.

Mice may abound in the grassy areas of our right-of-ways to the benefit of hawks and owls, some of which are becoming rare.

Many states and provinces allow rows of trees to stand along the edges of their highways for scenic purposes. If old pine trees are included, the Red-cockaded Woodpecker, a rare species, will benefit (within its range). The wider median strips of larger highways afford great opportunity for the development of habitat. Many of these have been planted with trees and shrubs of benefit to birds.

Although the development of habitat along our highways generally is useful to birds, there are circumstances under which it should not be done. For example, plantings on opposite sides of a narrow road will encourage birds to fly back and forth across the road where they will be killed by the traffic. A better plan is to stagger the plantings so that none of the groups are opposite one another. Or, plantings can be restricted to one side of the road.

Highway authorities have a number of things to consider when making plantations. They do not, for

Black-capped Chickadee, *Parus atricapillus.* Fearless, inquisitive, friendly, are some of the words used to describe chickadees. We have seven species in North America, and of these the Black-capped is the most widespread. To distinguish the various species by their appearance is not easy in every case (all have dark caps and throat patches), but their songs and calls are helpful. 13 cm. (5″)

Veery, *Catharus fuscescens.* Although we often think of the Veery as a bird of the swamps or bogs, it visits our suburbs during migration. We even hear it sing at this time. The song, which may be expressed as *veery-veery-veery-veery,* has a quality that is rich and vibrant. The notes seem to spiral downward in pitch as they fade away. 18 cm. (7″)

Scarlet Tanager, *Piranga olivacea* (female) This tanager can be found along the woodland edges, but it seems to prefer to live within the forest. In the Appalachian Mountains, I have found it in the midst of the mature forests in summer, and in the Midwest, I now find it primarily within the larger stands of timber such as oak and hickory. 18 cm. (7")

Red-bellied Woodpecker, *Melanerpes carolinus.* (female) In some parts of its range, this species lives by choice in heavily timbered river bottoms. In others parts, it may be found in more open stands of trees, either deciduous or coniferous. It constructs its nest at almost any height above the ground, in dead or partly dead trees. 24 cm. (9.5")

example, plant evergreens where ice will form in their shade and become a hazard to traffic. Neither do they plant nut or fruit trees where children will attempt to gather their fruits while dodging traffic. Problems of disease with nearby orchards and crop fields must be considered when they select their planting stock. Some plants will not do well where gas fumes are strong, and others will not tolerate drought.

Forest Habitat

Of all the bird habitats under consideration, the forest is the most challenging from the standpoint of management. As far as the birds are concerned, a forest is much more than trees. Below the trees are shrubs; entwined with the trees and shrubs are vines; below the shrubs are herbs and other ground cover; below the ground cover plants are decayed leaves and rotting wood; and below these is the topsoil. In the topsoil, in addition to its rock particles and organic matter, are such valuable forms as bacteria, fungi, and earthworms. Because the soil is porous and absorbs water quickly, the forest helps to maintain the water table. The trees and other plants absorb water and carbon dioxide and release oxygen into the air. The above account is sketchy, but it gives us an idea of the complexity of the management problem.

All parts of the forest are useful to birds. A forest with an understory is attractive to the Wood Thrush. Extensive and continuous woodlands are preferred by the Pileated Woodpecker. The interior portions of a forest will be used by the Worm-eating Warbler. The edges of a forest are especially appealing to a variety of bird species, although such birds may, on occasion, also use the interior. Forest openings attract the Ruffed Grouse. If two forests are connected by a long, narrow strip of trees, this will have a bearing upon the distribution of forest birds. Mixtures of deciduous and coniferous trees appeal to many species of birds, while one type or the other may separately have its own devotees. Coniferous trees appeal to Pine Warblers; deciduous trees appeal to Great Crested Flycatchers. Of the two types, it seems that the deciduous may attract the most species of birds.

Forests do not remain static. Because of plant succession they are constantly changing. On a continental basis, this usually does not seriously handicap the birds, but locally it can become a problem, and this is where management enters the picture.

Forestry Practices

Many forestry practices as we find them today are not a hinderance to birds if we consider them on a continental basis.

Ornithologists well know that diversified forests attract the greatest number and variety of birds. Thus selective cutting of trees can be a help to the birds. This method thins out a forest that may be too dense for some birds and admits light which will increase the growth of the younger trees and shrubs. If openings of moderate size are created as a result of selective cutting, the edge thus formed will be attractive to many bird species. Selective cutting often is limited to deciduous forests.

Clear cutting has both positive and negative effects on birds. On the one hand, those species that nest in openings are benefited, but those species that need the forest are adversely affected. Such management on the local level can disrupt or even terminate the ancestral lineages of certain species. It can be argued that many of these preempted birds may move into the nearby

Nashville Warbler, *Vermivora ruficapilla.* (female) The Nashville Warbler is a denizen of the cutover or second-growth forest where shrubs and other understory plants are plentiful. The habitat may be either moist or dry. The birds construct their nests on the ground, usually under a plant of some kind for protection. The nesting range is divided, very few birds being found in the area between Minnesota and Idaho. 13cm. (5″)

Wood Thrush, *Hylocichla mustelina.* The Wood Thrush is well named, for it is restricted mainly to the woodlands, especially to those that have a good understory of shrubs. It uses mud in the construction of its nest, so it usually settles down near water. In common with the robin, the Wood Thrush gets greatly excited if its nest is approached. 20cm. (8″)

Mourning Warbler, *Oporornis philadelphia.* (male) The Mourning Warbler inhabits second-growth forests, particularly the openings where brush is dense. Here it builds its nest on or near the ground, in either wet or dry situations. Wilson named the species for the dark spot (crepe) on its breast. He did not mean to imply that the species had a mournful cry. 14cm. (5.5″)

Canada Warbler, *Wilsonia canadensis.* (male) This warbler does a great deal of flycatching. Thus it affords the observer many glimpses, although it confines itself regularly to the undergrowth of wooded habitat. It nests on the ground. The breeding range spreads across much of Canada, but the species is seldom seen in the western half of the United States. 14cm. (5.5″)

forests, but experiments show that only a small percentage can do this. Presumably the neighboring forests are already claimed.

In some regions, it is only the coniferous forests that are clearcut. Such forests often do not lend themselves to selective cutting. Some wildlife workers express little regret when coniferous forests are clearcut, for they consider them to be "biological deserts." I do not agree with this thinking, although I can see why they reach this conclusion. The shade of a dense coniferous forest kills out most of the understory.

Foresters and lumbermen are subject to certain rules and customs, not all of which are favorable to birds. They may be required, for example, to cut down old snags along the "skid" roads and other work areas for safety's sake. Unfortunately, this may take all of them. Old snags thus eliminated, are not often replaced today as lumber is harvested on a short-rotation basis because of economic reasons. Moreover, some foresters object to dead trees because they harbor insects.

By the time the trees of the forest have reached their climax stage, the forest understory is fairly well shaded out, and this is one of the reasons why certain species of birds go elsewhere. With younger forest stands, not all foresters and lumbermen are agreed as to the value of the understory. Some like to eliminate it, while others like to keep it, at least around the edges of the forest. The former believe that the understory is a hinderance to the growth of trees; the latter believe that it will help to keep out drying winds.

Foresters and lumbermen raise trees as a crop. As with the farmer, they cannot prevent certain wildlife losses. In fact, they may take a dim view of wildlife in general, because certain species damage their trees.

As indicated above, lumber may be harvested

before the trees are fully grown. When we realize that it may take from seventy-five to one hundred and seventy-five or more years for a tree to grow to full size, we can understand why this is done. Today, efforts to hasten the growth of trees have been successful in some areas.

Although wildlife may be scorned by some lumbermen, there are a few cases on record wherein income derived from the presence of wildlife in the forest was greater than that attained from the sale of lumber.

Not all economic self-interests in forests are associated with lumbermen. Cattlemen have a role to play. The effects of grazing cattle can be seen in larger forests as well as in wood lots. When a forest is severely grazed, the understory is lost and this is hard on the birds. From the forester's standpoint, grazing cattle compact the soil to the detriment of tree growth. Some foresters believe that rather than to graze an entire wood lot, it would be better to sacrifice a part of the woods entirely, cut it down and devote the land to pasture. The remaining woods, though smaller, could then be fenced off.

Managing The Forests For Birds

Until recently, very little money has been made available for the management of nongame birds, but experience gained in the management of game species has been helpful. We are now in a position to manage the forests quite well for birds of many kinds. We know, for example, that a shrub border around the edge of a forest is of benefit to many species, and such a plan meets the approval of many lumbermen. Also the border can be further enhanced by underplanting its outer edge with food-bearing herbs and the like.

Dense stands of trees, especially the larger ones,

Ruby-crowned Kinglet, *Regulus calendula.* (female) The Ruby-crowned Kinglet is common in almost any kind of wooded or partly wooded habitat, but it shows a preference for conifers, particularly spruces, during its nesting season. It builds its nest in such trees at almost any height above the ground. The species is widespread in North America. 10cm. (4")

Bay-breasted Warbler, *Dendroica castanea.* (female) Bay-breasted Warblers may be observed in trees of all kinds, and at almost any height above the ground, but they favor the coniferous habitat during the nesting season. They often build their nests on the horizontal branches of fir trees. In general appearance, the female resembles the male, but her colors are pale by comparison, 14cm. (5.5")

Rufous-sided Towhee, *Pipilo erythrophthalmus.* (female) This towhee spends much of its time in the understory of the forest. It nests here and finds much of its food on the ground. Its overall nesting range (all forms) extends from the southern fringe of Canada, southward to parts of Central America. (My photograph was taken in Wisconsin.) 20 cm. (8″)

Hooded Warbler, *Wilsonia citrina.* (male) Hooded Warblers are birds of the forest understory. I have found them regularly in stands of mountain laurel in the Appalachian Mountains, and in thickets of Tartarian honeysuckle in the Midwest. The song of the male brings the birds to our attention. A typical rendition consists of seven syllables, the last three of which are rapidly rendered. 14 cm. (5.5″)

can be made more attractive to certain species of birds if a few openings are created. The size and number of these openings will vary with the size of the forest. The basic reason for providing these openings is to create additional edge where food-bearing plants can grow. Large blocks of timber are usually split up by means of firebreaks for obvious reasons, but these fire lanes also provide edge where food-bearing plants can be set out. Increased sunlight here gives the plants a boost. Although certain species of birds benefit from openings in the forest, others require the opposite. They enjoy the seclusion afforded by large, solid stands of timber.

Excellent habitat can be created for wintering waterfowl, especially Mallards and Wood Ducks, by temporarily flooding live timber. The potential water area does not have to be continuous, but it should be shallow. Before undertaking such a project, though, consideration should be given to the following questions: Will the soil hold water? Will you be able to drain the area again? Will the water flood more land than you plan to? Is the water supply ample to do the job? If the flooding is limited to the fall and winter seasons, it will not injure live trees. In fact, the extra moisture provided may serve to enhance tree growth. (Permits may be required to flood.)

Christmas tree plantations are very useful to the birds. Prairie Warblers, in particular, seem to like them, and I have found Clay-colored Sparrows in them on several occasions. Their use changes as the trees grow tall and also when trees are removed.

Often it is difficult to get nut trees started in areas where squirrels abound. One way to outwit them is to place an old tin can upside down over the nut. Before the can is used for this purpose, the bottom should be cut (slit) in the same way a pie is cut and the central points of the tin bent upward to allow the plant to grow up through the opening.

When a new forest of any kind is to be planted, a number of things need to be kept in mind. Are the trees adapted to the soil? Are they shallow-rooted or deep-rooted? Is the amount of annual rainfall sufficient? Is the climate agreeable? Will the trees grow on a northern slope? Do they require shade when they are young? How far apart should they be planted, and in what mixture? From the bird's standpoint, trees should be of various sizes and age. To accomplish this, a few can be planted each year until the project is completed. From the landowner's point of view, this could be a good idea too, as unfavorable weather, if it does come, would affect only a small part of the project.

Food-bearing trees, should always be given high priority in forest management for birds. Even when a forest is to be clearcut, a few of them can be allowed to stand. Trees that are dead should also be left standing if the laws permit. They furnish food for the woodpeckers and certain other species, and cavities built in them, or that are naturally formed in them, help a variety of birds. In forests where dead trees are not permitted to stand, bird houses can be employed. They are used this way in Europe with great success.

Fallen tree trunks also have many uses if left in the forest. Ruffed Grouse use them as drumming logs, and Pileated Woodpeckers find much of their insect food in them. Some birds like to construct their nests in the upturned roots of such trees. If freshly fallen trees, having branches, are left in place, they will protect the ground below from late freezes in the spring. I have flushed American Woodcock from such sheltered spots when the surrounding ground was frozen solid.

When a new forest is planted, the speed of growth

Northern Oriole, *Icterus galbula.* The oriole (male) illustrated here was, until recently, known as the Baltimore Oriole. Today, it is combined with what was formerly known as Bullock's Oriole, to constitute the Northern Oriole. The ranges of the two forms merge in the Great Plains, and there is some hybridization there. 19 cm. (7.5")

Wild Turkey, *Meleagris gallopavo.* (male) Wild Turkeys are birds of the wilderness. Forest stands with scattered openings in them are important. The latter provide a place to nest, and often a variety of food. Turkeys like to roost in trees, and to feed there if food is available. They may not be observed there, as they often leave such habitat before sunrise. Wild Turkeys may be identified by the brownish band on the tip of the tail. 122 cm. (48")

Acadian Flycatcher, *Empidonax virescens.* The Acadian Flycatcher is a bird of the forest understory. Curiously, its nesting range does not include Nova Scotia which was formerly known as Acadia. Its back is greenish-gray, but the best way to identify it is to hear its typical call. This sounds like *swee-up,* the second syllable being the highest in pitch. 14 cm. (5.5″)

Black-crowned Night-Heron, *Nycticorax nycticorax.* This heron reminds us that, although herons are seen often in marshes, they do feel at home in trees. In fact, many species, including the one illustrated here, nest in trees. Black-crowned Night-Herons eat such a variety of foods that they are not necessarily restricted to our wetlands. I have seen them nesting in the suburbs of cities. 66 cm. (26″)

is often paramount. One way to expedite this is to plant legumes such as clovers, beans, and locust trees. Legumes enrich the soil, and in the shade that the locust trees provide, shade-loving trees can get started. Some of the trees that need shade in this way are maples, beeches, basswoods, and hemlocks. If a deciduous forest is planned on acreage that is occupied by conifers, shade-loving trees can be planted in their shade before the conifers are removed.

In semiopen country where the existing trees are of the deciduous type, variety in bird life may be enhanced by planting a few clusters of coniferous trees. Badly grazed wood lots can be restored by planting some shade-tolerant shrubs and other plants. Erosion, if it has occurred, should be controlled.

River and Stream Habitat

To decide which part of a river or stream is most valuable to birds, or most interesting to ornithologists, is difficult. I like the mountain streams, especially those that are spring-fed. I am reminded of the Winter Wren which I have often heard singing along their edges. In the West, I think of the American Dipper, which spends much of its time in clear, cool water.

In areas where the waters of mountain streams slow down somewhat, beavers build their dams. Such water impoundments are useful to birds. Ducks raise their broods there. In the East, the American Black Duck, in particular, is fond of such waters. Other ducks that use them during the nesting season are Green-winged Teal, Ring-necked Duck, Common Goldeneye, Hooded Merganser, Wood Duck, and Mallard. Usage varies, depending upon the elevation of the site. In the West, Barrow's Goldeneye may replace the Common Goldeneye on some of the dams. Active beaver dams are more useful than those that have been abandoned. The usual cause for abandonment is the lack of suitable trees to cut, but beaver normally can keep their homes going for a period of seven to ten years. In some states, wildlife managers sow millet in the beds of beaver dams which have been abandoned to furnish food for the ducks. In other places, wildlife managers import beaver and stock them along the streams where they are needed. Some managers even furnish them with aspen (poplar) wood, one of their favorites.

Many mountain streams flow through areas that are well shaded, and this provides excellent habitat for fish. If they flow through sunny areas, especially in the lower elevations, their waters become too warm for certain species. To help offset this, fish managers often plant evergreen trees and shrubs along the stream banks to provide shade. Needless to say, such work is a great help to the birds. Fish managers also do many other things that aid the birds.

A stream or river is a thing of such natural beauty that many people hesitate to build dams on them. In addition to aesthetic considerations, the interests of the local people must be ascertained. No one disputes the fact that utility dams are needed, but how many and where to locate them creates the problem. On a continental basis, the utility dams we now have are no hinderence to birds. Locally, they may flood out certain desirable song bird habitats, but they compensate for this by providing habitat for water birds. Because the flow of water through the dam must be regulated to suit the business, its fluctuations may be a hinderance to nesting birds and other wildlife below the dam.

Water is often impounded for city reservoirs, and such reservoirs are usually not off limits for birds. Song birds often find ideal nesting habitat along the shores of

Winter Wren, *Troglodytes troglodytes.* I can still remember the first time I heard the song of this species. The bird was perched on the edge of broken ice, along the border of a flowing stream in the Appalachian Mountains. Its performance was in keeping with the trickling sound of the slow-moving water. Not many species have a continuous song of such length. 10 cm. (4″)

Swamp Sparrow, *Melospiza georgiana.* How do we get Swamp Sparrows for the Christmas Bird Count in the North? We *squeak* them out into the open. It's a fact! Otherwise, we can walk by a marsh repeatedly and never see a bird. Although called Swamp Sparrow, this species is a denizen of the open wetlands, as opposed to densely wooded swamps. 14 cm. (5.5″)

Wood Duck, *Aix sponsa.* (male) By nature Wood Ducks nest regularly in old woodpecker cavities and hollow trees. However, such accomodations are scarce in many places today, so wildlife managers and others have provided nest boxes for them. These boxes are placed in wetlands, usually where there are some trees. 48 cm. (19″)

Nest of Red-shouldered Hawk, *Buteo lineatus.* One young bird stands out clearly in my picture, but there were probably at least two more in the nest, as the species commonly lays three eggs (occasionally four). The nest tree was situated near a river, as is often the case with the Red-shouldered Hawk. While there, I noticed that the adults could really make the woodlands ring with their calls.

dams and reservoirs. Water birds use the waters as would be expected. One use, though, that may not be so widely known is that made of utility dams by Bald Eagles. Fish that make their way through the dams often are incapacitated or otherwise brought to the water's surface where the eagles can easily snatch them up. If conditions are favorable, the eagles may spend the winter in the vicinity of such dams. Wisconsin, for example, has several dams of this kind where the Bald Eagles gather in large numbers.

There are also side effects of such large water impoundments. Backwaters also are present, which generally form shallow or swampy water habitat for birds.

Construction Of Flowages

In order to provide good wetland habitat for birds in areas where it is scarce, shallow flowages often are constructed on streams or along rivers. Large-scale projects of this kind usually are handled by governmental agencies, but small flowages and farm ponds are often constructed by private individuals. Instructions, including laws, on how to go about this should be obtained locally as they will be tailored to fit the situations. A general idea of what is involved, however, will be useful to anyone who is interested in the welfare of birds.

Normally a permit is needed to impound water. This is required to protect the rights and interests of people in the neighborhood, but is important to the operator too, for it will inform him how to avoid some of the usual pitfalls. In some regions, financial help is also available.

Often an earthen dike will serve to impound the water, but a control device should be installed to regulate the outflow. The banks of the proposed water area should slope gradually toward the water, and the portion to be flooded should cover at least 1.2 heactares (3 acres). Of course, larger areas are still more useful. Unless fish are to be raised, it is best to keep the water shallow, that is, about 0.6 meters (2 feet) in the deeper parts. If a small island can be constructed in the center of the water area, it will further enhance its value, as waterfowl need resting spots where they will not be bothered by roving mammals.

In many parts of the land, especially in the South, the needed vegetation, both in and out of the water, may come up voluntarily. In fact, some plants may grow too densely to suit the birds. In those parts of the land where planting is necessary, duckweed, burreed, millet, and bulrush are some of the best for planting in the water area. They furnish food for waterfowl. When planting them, mix the varieties rather than group them in single stands. Also some parts of the water area should be left unplanted. If plants are needed along the banks, smartweed, rye, oats, barley, rice, and wheat are among those that will furnish food.

Farm ponds usually are not constructed primarily for birds and other wildlife, as cattle and other livestock require access to the water. This can be arranged, however, on a convenient part of the pond without disturbing the remainder.

A dependable water supply is needed if farm ponds and other small impoundments are to be of maximum value to birds. If a pond is allowed to dry up during the summer, ducks would be left in the lurch. There would be no water for the ducklings, and the parent birds, because of their annual molt, would not be able to fly elsewhere. If an area is suitable for ducks, boxes can be put up as a further inducement to them. I am here referring to such species as Wood Ducks and the others

Bald Eagle, *Haliaeetus leucocephalus.* On June 20, 1782, the Bald Eagle, commonly called the American Eagle, was selected by the United States Congress as the national emblem. It was regarded as a symbol of power and valor because of its majestic appearance in flight and dignity when at rest. Its head is not bald, but covered entirely with white feathers. 94 cm. (37")

Common Moorhen, *Gallinula chloropus.* This species, formerly called the Common Gallinule, breeds as far north as the latitude of the Great Lakes in the East, and northward to a limited extent, along our western coast. It is more active at night, or during twilight hours, than during the day, but it may be observed near cover when the sun is shining. 33 cm. (13")

King Rail, *Rallus elegans.* The expression, "thin as a rail," reminds us that all rails are able to run with ease between the stalks of cattails, rushes, or weeds that commonly make up their habitat. Thus they do not have to fly unless cornered. The King Rail, despite its size, follows the rules of the family, and keeps out of sight most of the time. 43 cm. (17")

Common Snipe, *Gallinago gallinago.* The Common Snipe has an elaborate aerial courtship performance. In quality, the sound comes close to what we boys in elementary school, used to make by swinging a ruler around on a short string. When the snipe performs, it usually is so high in the sky that the uninitiated cannot perceive the source of the sound. 28 cm. (11")

that nest in tree cavities.

Some people having ponds for waterfowl are so situated in the flyways that it would be helpful if they could prevent ice from freezing over the water. There is a way to do this by means of a pump and hose combination which is available on the market. It forces the warmer subsurface water up to the surface.

Many species of waterfowl prefer habitat for feeding that is different from their nesting habitat. Thus, if there is room, it may be feasible to create two flowages instead of one. Or, it may be desirable to create one large flowage with several small flowages around its edge.

In order to have an abundant food supply, a large flowage may be sown with seed by airplane. Depending upon the varieties to be planted, some may be sown upon the water in one part, and upon the wet ground in another, the latter having been drained for the purpose. Seeds should be prepared ahead of time as some kinds need to be soaked in water; some need to be scarified (cut); and others do best after they have been frozen. Some of the most popular plants to sow for later flooding are the various millets, buckwheats, and smartweeds. When these seeds are sown on drained wet soil, they produce a much more abundant crop then can be expected from plants growing in permanent water areas. This is not to say that permanent water areas should be left unplanted, for ingenious ways have been devised to set out live plants in water where, normally, they would be washed away. (Plants and methods of planting them vary geographically, so it is best to obtain instructions from the nursery that raises them.)

To be able to drain a flowage has more than one advantage. The soil below the water may need to be rejuvenated, certain undesirable plants may be growing rampant, or carp may be a nuisance. Whenever water levels are manipulated, care should be exercised not to destroy the nests and eggs of birds.

It is not possible to build dams or flowages on all rivers and streams. Some are kept open for navigation. Others do not carry enough water. Permits are not issued for the latter because evaporation is much more rapid over wide expanses of water than over narrow streams. If water were dissipated in this way, the people who live downstream could be deprived of their share.

Occasionally, workers find that the soil under the proposed flowage area will not hold water. Sometimes we hear the objection that mosquitoes will become a problem if wetlands are created. This can happen, but there are now several products on the market that will control them without doing damage to the environment. Opinions on such matters are subject to change, though, so it is best to check with the governmental agency that is responsible.

Natural Widespreads

As our rivers flow down into the lowlands, their character changes. Their banks often cannot contain the volume of water that accumulates, with the result that natural flowages are formed. In the South, many of these are wooded. The river delta also provides excellent habitat for birds. I think of our river deltas in the Arctic, in particular. What a spectacular variety of water birds they support!

In recent years, many of our rivers have been singled out as scenic rivers. These are to be preserved as well as possible in their natural condition.

Tricolored Heron, *Egretta tricolor.* Can herons run? The bird in the illustration tells us that they can run from photographers. It did not have to run, for herons are narrow in build and can squeeze between the reeds in order to hide. The heron shown here is not as well known as many of our species, for it is largely coastal in its distribution. 66 cm. (26")

Sandhill Crane, *Grus canadensis.* To many of us, the sight of a flock of Sandhill Cranes is very impressive, and if the birds are calling, the experience is one that will never be forgotten. We think of them as birds of the secluded marshes, and rightly so, for they do nest over, or near water. (I obtained my photograph at the International Crane Foundation.) 112 cm. (44")

Yellow-rumped Warbler, *Dendroica coronata* (male) The explanation for the above name lies in the fact that, recently, two forms (Myrtle and Audubon's) have been combined into one species. The form shown here is the Myrtle in fall plumage. It was so-named because it is fond of the berries of the wax-myrtle. The western form has a yellow throat. 14 cm. (5.5″)

Black-bellied Whistling-Duck, *Dendrocygna autumnalis.* This beautiful species, formerly known as one of our tree ducks, differs in various ways from what we would normally expect of ducks. Instead of alighting on the water, it often alights on land and walks to the water; and instead of swimming on the water to find its food, it commonly stands in its shallow edges. 53 cm. (21″)

Prairie Habitat

The vast area extending east to west from the Mississippi River to the Rocky Mountains, and north to south from central Alberta to southern Texas is commonly called the prairie region or Great Plains. Many widely scattered smaller areas also qualify as prairie land. The prairies were originally covered primarily with grasses of various kinds and their associates. Because the annual rainfall in the Great Plains is less than 51 cm. (20 in.) trees and shrubs did not find favorable growing conditions there, but the grasses, having relatively larger root systems, were able to grow. Even they grew sparingly in some of the drier spots. From the bird's point of view, the prairie was a great place, not only because of its grassland, but also because of its marshes.

Today a major portion of the original prairie is devoted to farming. When the Homestead Act was passed in 1862, farmers, upon making their claims, soon began to transplant trees from the river courses to the open prairie. This, of course, brought in certain new bird species. When the land was extensively farmed, further changes were inevitable. Cities which sprang up in the prairies also attracted species of birds that formerly would not have been expected.

Small parcels of the original prairie that remain today are in jeopardy because competing plants from the surrounding areas are moving in and soon will change the character of the land. Such unwanted plants are difficult to eradicate, except by prescribed burning. With careful planning, however, prairie land can be restored or even developed.

Farmers often favor birds by allowing prairie grasses, shrubs, and other small plants to grow along their fences and in the corners of the fields. If the shrubs are allowed to grow only on one side of the fence, they will not interfere with maintenance work. Trees are not desired here as they absorb too much moisture.

Some farmers have dispensed with fence construction and maintenance by using multiflora rose. Fencerows produced in this way will turn cattle, for multiflora rose grows thickly and is well equipped with sharp thorns. Also, it grows tall enough for the purpose. It can only be used in warmer regions, however, as it frostkills in the latitude to the north of Chicago. (Curiously, it does not do well in the latitude of Florida.) Those who use it say it is only a slight hinderance to crop production in the adjacent fields. Live fences of this kind are a great boon to birds, both as cover and as food. Multiflora rose hips are utilized by many species.

Those landowners who wish to include other food-bearing plants in their fencerows may try such shrubs as elderberry, bayberry, checkerberry, lespedeza, hazelnut, squawbush, dogwood, buffaloberry, viburnum, tamarisk, Russian olive, and pokeberry (in their respective ranges).

Sometimes we hear the complaint that fencerows habor injurious insects. No doubt, this is true at times and in certain regions, but the complaint is often exaggerated, for if we study the matter, we find that many of the insects found there are beneficial to man.

Farmers help birds in many ways. When land is allowed to lie fallow, for example, it furnishes nesting cover; and grain that falls by the wayside feeds many birds. Wildlife managers who raise food crops for birds and other wildlife, can handle crop land in a way entirely different from that used by the farmer who must make a living from it. For example, when a cornfield is planted, they can plant such things as Korean lespedeza, Ladino clover, soybeans, millet, milo, or whatever they wish between the rows, to furnish food for birds.

Gadwall, *Anas strepera.* (male) The Gadwall, sometimes known as the Gray Duck, is a bird of the marshes. It is restricted more to marshy habitat than the Mallard, for example, and this may explain why it is localized in it's distribution. Gadwalls, when on the water, appear to be rather nondescript in appearance, except that the males show clear black at the rear. 51cm. (20″)

Northern Pintail, *Anas acuta.* (female) The female of this species appears, from a distance, to be mostly brownish in color, but her plumage is mottled. Her nesting range in North America is vast, extending, as far north as the arctic tundra. It is interesting to note (from banding records) that some of our birds migrate to Hawaii for the winter. 56cm. (22″)

Marbled Godwit, *Limosa fedoa.* Marbled Godwits commonly feed in grass-covered prairie marshes, or in pools of shallow water where they can be easily seen. The bird, shown here, was photographed along the coast of Texas, during April. The name, *Godwit,* comes to us from the Old World; *marbled* describes the plumage. 46 cm. (18")

Burrowing Owl, *Athene cunicularia.* Burrowing Owls may be seen abroad during the day. When not looking for food, they often sit on the mounds of soil that they dig out of their burrows. In disagreeable weather, though, they may take refuge within their burrows. Today, all forms are included under the above caption. My photograph shows one of the dark forms. 25 cm. (10")

Pasture land, like crop land, can serve birds well. Moderate grazing can improve the habitat for Mountain Plover. When I was in Saskatchewan, I found Chestnut-collared Longspurs nesting in well-grazed meadows. Of course, it depends upon the system used and the kinds of animals involved. Goats are fond of shrubs, so they may not eat much grass. Sheep like a mixture of plants (commonly called forbs). Cattle and horses show a preference for grass. Many cattlemen use their pastures on a rotation basis, or they may allow first one kind of animal to use it, and later, another kind. Most of these methods give the birds a chance. Pastures, of course, can be overgrazed.

Wildlife managers have developed a rotation plan using native grasses such as switchgrass, Indian grass, and big bluestem. Grazing of this type of pasture is postponed until after the nesting season is about over. The cattle, in the meantime, use an alternate pasture. Further, the native grasses mentioned above are not grazed closely, but allowed to stand up well for the next nesting season, as many species of birds like to nest in the last year's growth. Cattle gain weight under this system, so it can be an improvement over the normal rotation plan.

Shelterbelts

Along with farming in the Great Plains came the problem of wind erosion. Great quantities of rich top soil have been blown away. Today, this kind of loss has been slowed down by means of shelterbelts (rows of trees). Coniferous trees are often used for this purpose because they are less demanding of the soil and its moisture than deciduous trees, and they have a generous supply of needles all year. Further, they have their longest branches near the ground where help is most needed. Pine, spruce, hemlock, fir, cedar, and holly (not a conifer) may be used, depending upon the climate and location. Some landowners prefer to use deciduous trees for this purpose, and when this is done, solid rows of shrubs are planted to provide density near the ground. Almost any kind of tree, native, or acclimated to the locality may be used. Not all operators plant the same number of rows of trees or shrubs. In some localities, one or two rows may be sufficient; in others, several rows may be needed. Ideas on this can best be obtained by checking out the performance of existing plantations in the neighborhood. Needless to say, shelterbelts are a great help to birds.

There are many other bonuses connected with this enterprise. Hot, drying winds can be slackened, thus enhancing the quantity and quality of crops in adjacent fields. Bees work best if they can be protected from strong winds. (This has application particularly in orchards.) The trees may also serve as snow fences. Snow, drifted against the rows of trees and shrubs, provides welcome moisture when it melts. Some agencies are planting rows of trees with the expectation that they will take the place of portable snow fences.

Planting stock for shelterbelts may be obtainable from certain governmental agencies at little cost. In fact, some states are now doing better than that. They are offering property tax exemptions to those landowners who plant new shelter belts of vegetation that prevent erosion and provide wildlife habitat.

Windbreaks

The custom of planting windbreaks to protect buildings has been applied for many years. It is conjectured that windbreaks can reduce the wind's speed by fifty percent. They are most effective if kept a proper

American Avocet, *Recurvirostra americana.* American Avocets are birds of the open marshes and other shallow-water areas. They do not attempt to hide, but stand in the most open places, sometimes in large flocks. When feeding, they sway from side to side, thus cutting the water continuously with their upturned bills. 46 cm. (18")

Henslow's Sparrow, *Ammodramus henslowii.* The presence of Henslow's Sparrows is usually indicated by their calls, for they keep out of sight most of the time. The song, the part we hear of it, sounds like *chis-lik,* with the accent on the first syllable, It carries well, so the singer may be farther away than expected. Curiously, this species sings also during the night. 13 cm. (5")

Blue Jay, *Cyanocitta cristata.* Those coniferous trees which man has planted for shelterbelts across the Great Plains have helped the Blue Jay, for it often uses them as nesting sites. If oak trees are nearby, they will help also, as the jay includes acorns in its diet. Some migration takes place seasonally, but there is no consistency as far as the individual is concerned. 30cm. (12")

Mourning Dove, *Zenaida macroura.* (male) Mourning Doves benefit by the planting of shelterbelts and windbreaks, especially in the Great Plains, as they prefer to nest in trees. When they nest on the ground, the young are more subject to predation. Their cooing is a welcome sign of spring to many people, but it must have sounded mournful to those who named the species. 30cm. (12")

distance away from the buildings, and this varies with the location of the site. A rule of thumb provides that the distance can be as much as twice the height of buildings to be protected. Details regarding the kinds of trees and shrubs and their arrangements are very similar to those described above for shelterbelts. Birds benefit greatly from windbreak plantations, and small fruit and vegetable gardens thrive with such protection.

Prairie Wetlands

As the prairies produce most of the grain raised on our continent, it is amazing that we still have room for wetlands. Unfortunately, the acreage remaining in wetlands is only about half of what it was originally. But if we can retain what we now have, we may do quite well. The preservation of wetlands, whether on the prairie or elsewhere, is not for the benefit of birds and other wildlife alone. Wetlands help to maintain a high water table, and plants growing therein help to purify the water. The latter applies to drinking water as well as to the waters of our rivers and streams. A high water table is valuable, especially in times of drought. Fortunately, it is more economical to rely upon wetlands for these services (they are a part of our natural environment), than upon technology.

Realizing that wetland preservation is in the public interest, governmental agencies in certain parts of our land are now paying landowners to save or enhance their wetlands. Hopefully all agencies will cooperate in this way in the near future. Wetlands have great scientific and recreational value, and products removed from them give our economy a boost.

Birds of all kinds, game and nongame, need wetlands. Until recently, nongame birds, including many water birds, had to ride along on the "coattails" of the game bird programs. Supporters of the latter were sportsmen. Ducks Unlimited, a private organization of sportsmen begun in 1937, has financed the rebuilding or establishment of hundreds of wetlands. Today, many governmental agencies have funds available for the benefit of nongame species.

Some of the most productive wetlands for birds are still located in the Northern Great Plains. Additional productive areas may be found in the Great Basin and other regions of the West. Melting snow furnishes much of the moisture needed. Those wetlands of the Northern Great Plains are subjected to drought conditions periodically as the annual rainfall is scant. When droughts run rampant, many of the breeding birds move a little farther north into the partially forested lands, but it is doubtful whether they can hold their own indefinitely in this way. There is one plus factor in prolonged drought, however—the marsh has a chance to rehabilitate itself.

Management Of Wetlands

Although large organizations and governmental agencies are in the best position to work on wetland projects, private individuals or small groups do, on occasion, seek to restore or establish wetlands.

In some regions, financial or other kinds of help can be obtained from governmental agencies. Some of these agencies furnish plants for the purpose at low cost; most can furnish the "know-how."

If puddle ducks, such as Mallards, are wanted, the water should be relatively shallow; if diving ducks, such as Canvasbacks, are wanted, the water should be quite deep. All wetlands serve best if the edges can be shallow. Vegetation should be varied in size, kind, and distribution. Large areas serve well, but there is some

Canvasback, *Aythya valisineria.* (female) The back of the female is darker than that of the male, and her head, neck, and breast plumage is brownish. However, she can be easily recognized by her flat-headed appearance. The female Redhead, which has an abrupt forehead, sometimes lays her eggs in the nest of the Canvasback. 56 cm. (22")

Caspian Tern, *Sterna caspia.* The Caspian Tern, named for the sea of the same name, is our largest tern. In general, it resembles the Royal Tern, but its bill is red instead of orange, and its tail is less forked. Further, its forehead does not turn white during the winter season. Its breeding range covers much of North America. 53 cm. (21")

Long-billed Curlew, *Numenius americanus.* Within its breeding range, the Long-billed Curlew feels at home in old pasture land, wet meadows, and the like; but in migration, it visits beaches and other sites where water is available. (I took my photograph in southern California.) The species may be seen in flocks, occasionally, particularly in the West. It is named for its call. 61cm. (24″)

Yellow Warbler, *Dendroica petechia.* (male) The males are tireless singers. In the Midwest, we look for them in damp habitat that is partly covered with low-growing shrubs. They may be the same individuals year after year as they have a strong homing instinct. (We have several forms of the Yellow Warbler; the male shown here was photographed in Wisconsin.) 13cm. (5″)

advantage in creating several small areas, if the terrain is suitable. Certain species of ducks like to nest at some distance from their feeding or resting territories. More edge can be provided with several small water areas than with one large area. If a large area must be retained, its edges can be lengthened by the construction of irregular shorelines, thereby accomodating more birds.

Do not hesitate to modify or redo wetlands that appear to be on the wane, for no wetland retains its prime condition indefinitely; however, wetlands that traditionally dry up in summer, should be reconstructed or discontinued.

One quick way to modify or deepen a marsh is by blasting. Pothole blasting can be done, under the proper permits, with a mixture of ammonium nitrate and fuel oil. Instructions should be obtained when the permit is applied for. Another quick way to alter a marsh is by means of prescribed burning. That is, careful planning should precede the burn. Unwanted vegetation, both over the water and on the surrounding land can be cleared in this way, and ashes from the fire will be a help to the new plants. Bear in mind that the direction of the wind might change after the fire is started. Never allow the peat to be burned.

Grazing by cattle, while normally a great hinderance, can be planned in a way to improve the habitat around a marsh.

New species of birds may be expected to respond quicky to well-planned change. On the other hand, species that have a strong homing instinct may be squeezed out of their former haunts by noticeble change. All planning should be done with certain bird species in mind.

Trees are not wanted as a general rule in the vicinity of a prairie waterfowl marsh. Unwanted animals sometimes become a problem around wetlands. Some operators feel so strongly about this that they install electric fences around their marshes. Many of these animals can be trapped or hunted during the open seasons. On the other hand, muskrats and nutria can improve habitat by eating out or thinning unwanted vegetation, and their homes are often used as nesting sites by various species of water birds. Carp (not a native fish) should never be allowed to become established in the waters.

Other Habitats

One of the most interesting habitats is the arctic tundra. It is unbelievably important to the birds, although at first glance, it may seem to be one of the most inhospitable. The ground is frozen, except for a few inches of topsoil that may thaw out during the summer. This, in turn, remains wet for the most part, as drainage is poor and evaporation slow. Sedges, forbes, lichens, mosses, and the like grow here during the long daylight hours of the short summer season. Most of our water birds are represented here during the breeding season. There is ample water for them, especially along and near the coasts, the river deltas in particular, playing a dominent part. In addition, many species of song birds make the arctic region their summer home. Preservation of the arctic tundra as it exists today would seem to be in order. Already refuge areas have been established in some parts of the arctic.

Immediately to the south of the arctic tundra is a broad band of habitat which I like to call the taiga. It is mostly quite barren, but trees, stunted in size, may be found in the valleys. In some parts, bogs predominate, and water birds may concentrate there. Overall, it is a valuable habitat for birds. No doubt much of it will be

Snow Goose, *Chen caerulescens.* For many years, the Blue Goose and Snow Goose were regarded as separate species, but today, they are combined under the above caption. The blue form is more limited in its range than the other, both in summer and in winter. It nests in the arctic tundra from Baffin Island to Keewatin, and winters in selected parts of our eastern and gulf coasts, including parts of Mexico and the West Indies. The white form nests in the arctic tundra from Greenland to Alaska, and southerly into the Hudson Bay area. Its winter range also is comparatively large as it takes in the western coast from southern British Columbia to Baja California, in addition to the selected parts of our eastern and gulf coasts as described for the blue form. Both forms are geese of medium size. 71 cm. (28")

Gray-cheeked Thrush, *Catharus minimus.* Nests of this thrush may be found in either coniferous or deciduous growth, depending upon the geographical range. In the taiga, the nests are constructed at a distance of only a few feet above the ground as the trees are stunted here. Their wintering grounds are in northern South America, so the birds must travel long distances twice a year. 19 cm. (7.5″)

Blackpoll Warbler, *Dendroica striata.* (female) The nesting range of this species includes some of the most inhospitable habitat of the far North. The birds build their nests on the ground where there are no trees. We know the species as a late migrant, for it has a long distance to travel from its winter range in South America. The female lacks the clear-cut black crown of the male, for which the species is named. 14 cm. (5.5″)

preserved. Incidentally, habitat similar to that found in the arctic tundra and in the taiga is found at high elevations in the mountains.

Areas of scattered trees, known as savanna, are very useful to many species of birds, such as Orchard Oriole, Warbling Vireo, and American Robin. Usually, it is not necessary to develop such habitat for birds, as it seems to come with civilization.

Deserts are hosts to birds which are somewhat specialized. In Africa, I have heard that the ostrich can survive dehydration better than some of the mammals. In our Southwest, some birds avoid the heat of the day by entering ground burrows. Others enter old woodpecker cavities found in the saguaro cacti. The walls of these cavities harden with age and make desirable sites. Apparently desert birds are able to protect their eggs from the intense heat of the day. Many species of birds take up residence along waterways where there is usually some vegetation. Today, a start has been made to preserve some of this habitat. Offroad vehicles however, remain a threat to some deserts. Cities in desert regions serve as oases for birds, but some of the species found here are not of the desert.

The southern tip of Florida is unique in having subtropical climate, so it can boast of birds seldom found farther north. The Everglades, which form a large part of this region, had become overly dry for several years because the waters of the Kissimmee River, which originally flowed into it, were diverted elsewhere. I understand that the state government has now decided to restore this supply of water.

In many parts of the land, wooded swamps are being preserved as refuges for wildlife. This is probably the best solution in this case, as it is often impractical to develop such habitat. Of course, management may be needed, depending upon the requirements of the species to be protected.

Many migratory birds spend the winters in tropical countries that are heavily populated with the economically poor. Thus much excellent habitat which our birds have been using is now needed for crop production. The World Wildlife Fund, in its campaign for migratory birds, is trying to find solutions to these problems.

The southern seacoasts are important to birds, as they host tremendous flocks of waterfowl in winter, and because of their relatively mild temperatures, permit certain species of song birds to spend the season farther north than otherwise. Along the seacoasts farther north, many pelagic birds find nesting sites in the rocky cliffs and on the neighboring islands. Not everything is harmonious along the coasts, as food supplies for geese, for example, are so scarce in some of the coastal marshes that game managers have resorted to burning off the upper vegetation in order to expose the rootstocks and tender shoots which the geese require. Inasmuch as habitat along the seacoasts is subject to abuse, considerable legislation has been passed to protect and preserve it. No doubt, this will continue.

Certain pest plants have to be controlled as a help to water birds. The water chestnut from the Old World is a hinderance to larger species, especially in Chesapeake Bay. A plant from India, called "hydrilla," now cloggs many rivers in the Southeast; and the water hyacinth from South America clogs lakes and rivers to the detriment of other forms of aquatic life. It should be noted, however, that the latter plant is not wholly a pest. It is used to clean waste water, and some cities are now growing it for this purpose.

The oceans furnish habitat for species of birds that

Warbling Vireo, *Vireo gilvus.* I have found Warbling Vireos in primitive habitat, but they seem to be attracted more regularly to villages, parks, and resort grounds—places of scattered trees. They construct their nests high in such trees, often the taller ones. The species has the most widespread nesting range of all our vireos. 14 cm. (5.5")

Brown Pelican, *Pelecanus occidentalis.* Brown Pelicans range year-round from South America, northward through Central America, Mexico, and the West Indies, to that part of our coast from Texas to North Carolina on the East, and to California on the West. The bird shown here is in immature plumage; I photographed it in March. 132 cm. (52")

Roseate Spoonbill, *Ajaia ajaia.* The rose color for which the species is named, is most pronounced in the wings and on the belly, but there is also a little cluster of it on the front of the breast. The species may be found year-round in South America, Central America, Mexico, the West Indies, and the southern tips of Florida, Louisiana, and Texas. 79 cm. (31")

Northern Flicker, *Colaptes auratus.* (female) The nest cavity of the Yellow-shafted form of the above named species may be excavated in aged trees of almost any species, and at almost any height above the ground. Often these cavities are in habitat that is largely open. (My picture illustrates the female of the Yellow-shafted form.) 33 cm. (13")

rarely come to land, except to nest. Food for these birds is not evenly distributed, as ocean currents vary in temperature and motion. To control pollution of the ocean is now a goal.

Concluding Remarks

Habitat management for the welfare of birds is currently carried on by governmental agencies, other organizations, and by private individuals. Many individuals work on habitat improvement projects without pay. I am confident that this will continue. Today, however, financial renumeration or incentive is available to workers in some localities. Utility companies, for example, may be able to obtain financial assistance from the government to create or maintain wildlife habitat under their high lines. They, in turn, will pay landowners to do the work. (There are certain rules which must be followed.) No doubt, there are other areas in which financial assistance is available.

Birds have peculiarities that make their management difficult. Unlike plants, they do not have to stay in an area unless they want to. If we succeed in building up a habitat that is favorable to one species, it may be at the expense of another. Some species do not use the same type of nesting habitat throughout their range. Other species will not tolerate the presence of man. Therefore, our efforts will never be one hundred percent successful. Nevertheless, the management of habitat is our key to success, for birds must have food and cover.

Chapter 7

SOME ASPECTS OF BIRD HUNTING

Sportsmen have played a vital role in the preservation of the birds of North America. Because of their interest, the management of birds is now on a sound footing. It is through their financial contributions that governmental wildlife agencies have been able to function. It is also through their help that much wildlife habitat has been preserved. Such help is far reaching because it not only aids the game species—it also provides help for the nongame species, the native plants, and so on.

Sportsmen hunt primarily for recreational purposes. Most of it is done with the gun, but bow hunting is gaining in popularity. Hunting with a falcon, one of the oldest forms, is limited to specialists.

It is unfortunate that hunting, as it was done (largely unregulated) during the early history of our country, still lingers in our minds, for it handicaps the true sportsman of today. Wild game can be managed as an annual crop without damage to the breeding stock so to harvest it is natural. If certain species of wildlife, including some bird species, were not removed in this way, we would have to control them in some other way because of crop damage problems.

Public Hunting Grounds

One of the most perplexing problems for today's sportsman is where to hunt. A small percentage of hunters have made themselves unpopular with private landowners with the result that all must suffer. Thus governmental agencies have established hunting grounds which are open to anyone who desires to use them.

Wire Saucer. Nests built in trees by Mourning Doves are frail in structure and subject to destruction by strong winds. Thus wildlife managers have designed a wire saucer (of hardware cloth) which can be attached to forks in trees. The saucer is 25 cm. (10″) in diameter. It may be attached from 2 to 6 m. (8 to 20 ft.) above the ground, preferably in shade. Habitat may be varied.

Common Moorhen, *Gallinula chloropus.* The bird shown here has not yet acquired its red frontal shield, but it may be recognized by its side stripe of white. In common with certain other marsh birds, it nods its head forward and backward while swimming, and flicks its short tail when walking. Thus it is easily identified. 33cm. (13″)

Canvasback, *Aythya valisineria.* (male) Many years ago when this species was named, canvas must have been paler in color, for the back of the male Canvasback appears to be virtually white when seen from a distance. In profile, the Canvasback appears to be somewhat flat-headed, as the slant of the forehead seems to be a continuation of the bill. 56 cm. (22″)

Canada Goose, *Branta canadensis.* Today many forms are included under the above caption, but all have white cheeks, black necks, and brownish bodies. The goose shown here is one of the smaller forms, historically known as the Cackling Goose. The honking produced by the latter, of course, is weaker than that of the larger forms. 58 cm. (23″)

Such areas may be labeled variously, depending upon their location; and some may be combined with fishing. Not all such land is publicly owned—it would be too expensive—but considerable acreage is leased. Public hunting grounds serve a good purpose if they are not too crowded with hunters. Without them, sportsmen fear they might be forced to adopt the Old World practice of limiting hunting to a chosen few.

Public hunting grounds serve as demonstration areas for private individuals who want to set up hunting areas of their own. (This will be discussed later.) During the nonhunting season, public hunting grounds have great value to naturalists, including researchers. Some agencies permit field trials to be held on these lands.

Raising Game Birds

Raising game birds is an ancient art. Reasons vary, but today the majority of those raised are for hunting purposes. Governmental agencies generally take the lead, raising and releasing large numbers every year. They also are likely to have the best "know-how." When private individuals wish to raise birds or other wildlife, they must acquire a permit. The work is highly specialized.

Some game farm operators spend considerable time trying to raise species that are becoming rare for release into the wild. Others devote their attention to such common species as pheasants, quail, and Mallards as they are comparatively easy to raise. Those birds released into the wild are usually banded. When they are shipped, they must be identified and crated in conformity with the laws. Some birds are sold for immediate use as food.

Releasing Game Birds Into The Wild

Game birds are released only under permit. Sportsmen's clubs and operators of private hunting areas stock only those species which are allowed by law. The reasons for this are easily understood. For example, we would not want to see a new species introduced if it would compete strongly with native species. It would not do to have a new bird disease inadvertently brought in from a foreign country, or to have a species with an insatiable appetite for farm crops. This is not to say that new species should never be introduced. On the contrary, after careful studies have been made, suitable species can be stocked with confidence. The search for them continues.

Populations of existing species also need supplementary help occasionally. Then, stocking is in order. Discretion is needed, for the basic problem may be the condition of the habitat. If the latter has deteriorated, no amount of stocking will increase the breeding stock, for all habitats have a saturation point. Once the habitat has been built up, the species in question will likely restore its own numbers and stocking will not be required. The odds for greater populations favor the wild birds which are found there now, as pen-reared birds, when stocked, have less stamina. Large numbers of pheasants are stocked on a "put-and-take" basis. There is no hope that they will serve to increase the permanent population. They are simply released for immediate shooting.

Winter Feeding of Upland Game Birds

This subject has been "kicked around" more than any other phase of game management. Some managers believe that winter feeding is useless if the habitat is poor, and if the habitat is good, there will be plenty of natural food. Other managers believe that artificial help

Greater White-fronted Goose, *Anser albifrons.* This goose is predominantly grayish-brown in color, but it is white about the base of the bill, and for this mark the species is named. The underparts are paler than the upper, and blotched irregularly with dark bars. (Immatures lack the white face and dark bars of the adult.) 76cm. (30")

Brant, *Branta bernicla.* This arctic breeder migrates southward for the winter and may be seen along our East Coast from the New England States to North Carolina, and along our West Coast from southern British Columbia to Baja California. (Inland records are rare.) Our western form differs in color from our eastern form, the median portion of the underparts being dark. 61cm. (24")

Eurasian Wigeon, *Anas penelope.* (male) This Old World species has been known in North America for many years. It nests regularly in Iceland and Siberia, so we may be getting birds from both directions. In the male, the pattern of the plumage is similar to that in the male American Wigeon, but the colors are different. Notably, the crown is buffy instead of white. 48 cm. (19")

American Wigeon, *Anas americana.* (male) Until recently, this species was known as the Baldpate. The forehead and crown area of the male is white in color (not bald). It was a good name as the white crown does distinguish the male. The species is well-known as it ranges over the greater part of North America during migration. 51 cm. (20")

is of considerable value. Perhaps it depends upon how the work is conducted.

The thought of "toting" heavy bags of grain back into the hinterlands where the game birds live, during subzero weather, does not appeal to the average sportsman. Moreover, he rationalizes that the landowner may not give him permission to go in. So he is tempted to unload his grain near the highways where the House Sparrows and pigeons will steal it, and where the traffic may kill those few game birds that are in the neighborhood.

I am confident that the most efficient way to feed game birds in winter is to develop patches of food plants which can be left standing throughout the season. Such patches could include berry- or nut-bearing plants as well as grain. Arrangements for this can be made in advance with the landowner. Naturally, such work would be done on those lands where one expects to hunt.

Sometimes we hear the plea that game birds should be fed at least in emergencies—after severe ice storms and the like. Actually, both Gray Partridges and Chukars can go without food for several days, Wild Turkeys for a week, and Ring-necked Pheasants for more than two weeks, to furnish a few examples. Grit, though, which many game species require, is likely to be in short supply during snowy weather.

Realizing that sportsmen in some localities may feel justified in undertaking a winter feeding program involving the use of grain, I will present the following discussion: Corn, buckwheat, sunflower seed, soybeans, wheat, rye, barley, millet, flax seed, cracked acorns, mill screenings (weed seed), and grit may be carried out into the field for this purpose. If feeding stations are widely scattered, squirrels and other grain eaters, as well as predators of the birds themselves, will be less likely to gather and make themselves a nuisance. Sometimes sportsmen build lean-tos or other shelters for their food offerings. When this is done, several escape holes should be left through which the birds can fly or run when danger threatens. If feeding programs are begun, they must be continued throughout the winter as the birds will become dependent upon the artificial supply. As several species do not care for dry grain, the growing of food-bearing plants (see Appendix B) is wise.

Feeding programs should always be conducted in conformity with local laws. This may have special application with reference to waterfowl, doves, and certain other species.

Special Hunting Areas

Commercial hunting grounds have been a boon to sportsmen. They may be called shooting preserves, pheasant preserves, game farms, or something else equally inviting to the hunter. Pheasants usually are featured, but some enterprises have Mallards for pass-shooting, or certain other kinds of game. Preserves may be operated by private individuals or by associations and may be open either to members only or to the public. Up-to-date lists of game preserves are obtainable from governmental agencies.

The fee for hunting may cover such things as dogs, guns, guides, meals, lodging, transportation, and, of course, the game that is furnished. A reasonable bag is assured as a rule, and the hunting season usually is longer there than elsewhere. Commercial hunting grounds are operated under permit. Those sportsmen who are interested in starting a new one may obtain instructions from the nearest governmental agency that is empowered to issue the permit.

Chukar, *Alectoris chukar.* Chukars, sometimes referred to as Rock Partridge or Red-legged Partridge, have become established locally in the area from eastern Montana and northern New Mexico on the east, to southern British Columbia and northern Baja California on the west. They are from the Old World, but not from a single locality. 30 cm. (12″)

Cinnamon Teal, *Anas cyanoptera.* This western species has many of the characteristics of the Blue-winged Teal. Both sexes have a wing pattern similar to that of the Bluewing. Otherwise, the male Cinnamon Teal appears to be mostly cinnamon-red in color. The female cannot be readily distinguished from the female Bluewing. In nesting and feeding habits, the two species agree quite well. 41 cm. (16″)

Blue-winged Teal, *Anas discors.* (female) The females of this species, when at rest, can be mistaken for female Green-winged Teal (brownish), unless a bit of the blue wing can be seen; and they resemble female Cinnamon Teal so closely that neither can be easily distinguished without their escorts. 41 cm. (16")

Canada Goose, *Branta canadensis.* To those of us who live in the North, the Canada Goose is a welcome sign of spring. It moves northward as rapidly as the ice melts on our rivers and marshes. The nesting range is broad, and many of the birds migrate as far north as the arctic tundra. 99 cm. (39")

The Trophy

One of the nice things about hunting is the trophy that can be preserved. As this will be kept in one's possession during the closed season, a permit will be required. The taxidermist is also required to possess a suitable permit to work on it.

Those sportsmen who have an artistic flair often spend considerable time whittling decoys or birds for ornamental purposes. These can be made either three-dimensional or flat. Any kind of wood desired may be used, but pine is one of the favorites. In order to make them lifelike, the most time should be spent on the head and neck, and when the subject is painted, the eyes should be left until last, for this is where the bird's personality is centered. Use paint that will not run.

Popular Game Species

Examples of popular game species are as follows:

Ruffed Grouse

The Ruffed Grouse, called partridge in some localities, is a bird of the forest. It is not uniformly distributed, but largely restricted to the semi-open pockets where the vegetation is varied. During the breeding season, its chicks are likely to be near water if there is any in the vicinity. Low vegetative growth usually hides them from view. The nest itself may be in more open woods and often at higher elevations. The chicks eat many insects but the adults feed on the buds, leaves, and fruits of trees, shrubs, and other vegetation. Food supplies usually are ample, though their nesting habitat may be in need of management. The most common problem is overgrazing by cattle. A bare understory will not do, especially in small woodlands. Ruffed Grouse are essentially sedentary in habit.

Sharp-tailed Grouse

The feeding habits and habitat requirements of this species are more varied than those of the Ruffed Grouse. The Sharp-tailed Grouse is a bird of the edge—where the forest meets the open or semiopen grassland. Much open grassland is required, and the grass and associated plants need to be of various heights and densities. How to preserve, restore, or improve the habitat of the Sharp-tailed Grouse will be apparent when an area is inspected. Perhaps all that will be necessary is to cut down a few trees. Food supplies generally are ample in most parts of the range.

American Woodcock

The key to woodcock management appears to be the presence of earthworms. In some ways, the woodcock's habitat is similar to that of the Sharp-tailed Grouse, but it is likely to be wetter. The nests usually are situated in woodland edges, forest openings, and in brush. The males do their aerial courtship or territorial dances high over open prairie or prairielike grounds, usually near the nesting site. Woodcock are migratory.

Ring-necked Pheasant

As pheasants live primarily on farm lands, their greatest problem is to find a safe place to nest. They like hay fields for this purpose, but unfortunately, hay-making time often comes before the eggs are hatched. Consequently, many nests are lost annually. The solution to this problem on a country-wide basis is difficult to find, but landowners may help by supplying cover for nesting purposes in out-of-the-way places that will be just as appealing to the birds.

In the colder parts of the pheasant's range, winter survival is a problem. By preference, the birds seek

American Woodcock, *Scolopax minor.* At close range, the woodcock may look like one of the oddities of Nature, but it is in no sense of the word a freak. Those great eyes, set so high in the head, enable it to see behind while feeding, and that long bill, equipped with an upper mandible, the tip of which can be operated like a flexible lip, enables it to probe deeply into the soil for its principal food, the earthworm. 28 cm. (11")

Common Snipe, *Gallinago gallinago.* The Common Snipe is a bird of the muddy shores of open lakes and marshes. If flushed, it flies away in a zigzag manner, calling as it goes. This call reminds me of the *squish* a person makes when walking through sticky mud. The bird's need for unfrozen soil is reflected in the extent of the winter range. 28 cm. (11")

Blue-winged Teal, *Anas discors.* (male) Bluewings are found frequently in the company of Northern Shovelers, Mallards, and other puddle ducks, usually in shallow water. Both sexes have broad areas of pale-blue on the forepart of the wing, and these marks stand out prominently in flight when the birds are viewed from above. During the spring, paired birds chirp a great deal when in flight, thereby making their presence known. 41 cm. (16")

American Wigeon, *Anas americana.* (female) As can be seen in the photograph, the female of this species is not conspicuously colored. In fact, she can be lost in a flock of ducks while feeding with them. American Wigeons are surface feeders, so much so, that if they want to feed on plants that grow in deep water, they wait until a diving bird brings them up. 51 cm. (20")

shelter in cattail marshes and the like during winter, but these marshes are not evenly distributed. Windbreaks, constructed widely in recent years, often serve quite well for winter protection. Food supplies generally are not a problem as the chicks eat a variety of insects, including grasshoppers; and the adults eat weed seeds, small grains, and wild fruits. Pheasants are sedentary in habit.

One thing that concerns wildlife managers greatly is why this species will not thrive in all parts of the land. Some believe that the problem is in the soil. As pheasants are polygynous, only a few males are needed during the breeding season. In fact, excess numbers of males may be a hinderance to the females at this time. Thus hunting seasons usually are established on males only.

Gray Partridge

The Gray Partridge, also known as the Hungarian Partridge, likes farm land. It can survive on land that is relatively bare. Nests are situated in grassy areas, so many face the same hazards as those of pheasants. When placed in hay fields, they are likely to be near the edges, and this is to their advantage in some cases. In winter the birds can find shelter by diving into the loose snow. They will also avail themselves of the protection afforded by windbreaks and the other shelter around a farm. The chicks feed on insects, and adults rely on weed seeds and small grains. Gray Partridges are sedentary.

Northern Bobwhite

Most of the nests I have found of the Northern Bobwhite have been in grass-weed mixtures. Some have been in brushy areas and others in open spots. As the bobwhite is a bird of the farm land, it is subject to hazards found there. Sometimes it resorts to open woodlands, and in some localities, prefers them. Mixed habitat is most favorable to it on a year-round basis. Small seeds constitute its principal diet, and these may include weed seeds, grass seeds, and small grain. Usually food is available; it's the quality of the habitat that may be lacking when bobwhites disappear. Further, they cannot stand severe winter climate, so their range is limited. They are sedentary in habit.

Wild Turkey

As the result of much effort on the part of wildlife managers, Wild Turkeys are now widespread. This is also due to the birds' ability to adapt themselves to habitat that varies geographically. In general, though, woodlands are important. In order to make successful releases of birds into new territory, wild stock is used, and this is introduced immediately prior to the nesting season.

Wild turkeys are nonmigratory, but they move about a great deal when looking for food. Their nests are concealed, often under thickets or the branches of fallen trees. The poults and the adults eat insects and other small animal life, but the adults depend largely upon acorns, other nuts, berries, pine seeds, small grains, seeds of grasses and weeds, and "greens." They prefer to roost in trees that are tall, and if these are standing in water, so much the better.

Wood Duck

Wood Ducks are often found in wooded bottomland—the kind commonly known as slough. They also like open marsh if suitable nesting trees or boxes are available nearby. They are able to take their ducklings to

Wild Turkey, *Meleagris gallopavo.* We commonly think of Wild Turkeys as birds of the warmer parts of our continent, but they can tolerate snow, and they do range as far north as the latitude of the Great Lakes. They eat a variety of foods, including acorns, thornapples, ragweed seeds, worms, and grasshoppers, so they do well in wilderness habitat. Male is 122 cm. (48″); female is 91 cm. (36″)

Northern Bobwhite, *Colinus virginianus.* (male) Northern Bobwhites do best where the habitat is varied. They often build their nests on the ground where herbaceous vegetation will conceal them. In fact, they draw the surrounding plants over the nest so that the eggs cannot be noticed from above. The birds require protection also in winter, so thickets of brush and forbs are needed. 25 cm. (10″)

Northern Pintail, *Anas acuta.* (male) This species is named for the long, thin, central tail-feathers of the male, and is sometimes called the sprigtail. This streamlined tail, and the gracefully-curved neck give the male a distinctive appearance. It is a surface feeder, and rides buoyantly on the water. Its range includes parts of the Old World. 71 cm. (28″)

Redhead, *Aythya americana.* (male) In most discussions about the Redhead, someone is sure to mention the Canvasback. Often the two species are found together, both nest on the prairies, and there is considerable resemblance in color; however, the Redhead has an abrupt forehead to distinguish it from the Canvasback. When winter arrives many Redheads resort to our sea coasts. 56 cm. (22″)

water, even though their chosen nesting sites are in the uplands. They do prefer some seclusion from man.

As Wood Ducks are cavity nesters, many sportsmen build nest boxes for them. When doing this, it is well to obtain the latest house designs from the nearest governmental agency, for predators can easily offset any gains made in this direction. As of this writing, no plan has been devised that is entirely satisfactory under all circumstances, so pick the plan that seems to be the most predator-proof for your proposed sites. (Common Goldeneyes, Buffleheads, and Hooded Mergansers are among the other species of ducks that will use similar houses.) Wood Ducks obtain aquatic plants and small animal life when feeding in the water. When on land, they find acorns and other nuts, seeds, and a variety of insects.

Mallard

The Mallard often nests on dry land, and seemingly by choice in grassy areas. Of course, such locations are usually near water. Mallards, perhaps because of their great numbers, are not as choosy as most ducks about their habitat, but may be found in the vicinity of water areas of almost any size. They eat a variety of foods, depending upon the season and the habitat. Most of it is vegetable, but some insect and small animal life is included. Grain and seeds of wild plants are important in winter. Aquatic plants of many kinds are utilized when available. The greatest help the sportsman can render this species is to preserve our wetlands.

Hunting Seasons

In recent years, hunting has been permitted of birds such as coots, cranes, doves, ducks, gallinules, geese, grouse, partridges, pheasants, ptarmigan, quail, rails, snipe, swans, turkeys, and woodcock.

It is understood that all sportsmen will acquaint themselves with the species to be hunted before they go afield, learn all the laws as they apply to their localities, avoid trespassing, consider the safety of people who may be nearby, and work patiently with the young hunter.

Wood Duck, *Aix sponsa.* (male) During the summer, the male Wood Duck loses its colorful plumage, and takes on what is known as the eclipse plumage. This causes the bird to resemble the female in general color, but this does not last very long. The male is able to migrate southward during the fall season. 48cm. (19")

Mallard, *Anas platyrhynchos.* Perhaps the Mallard is our best-known duck. It does well in the wild, and when convenient, it takes up residency in the suburbs of cities. The males have very little to say, but the females let their presence be known by their loud quacking. The well-known green on the heads of the males may look purple, depending upon the direction of the light. 58cm. (23")

Falcated Teal, *Anas falcata.* (male) The Falcated Teal, an Asiatic species, has been recorded in southwestern Alaska. It is considerably larger than the Green-winged Teal, and both sexes have crests. The species is named for the curved (falcated) feathering in the wing of the male. 48 cm. (19″)

Mute Swan, *Cygnus olor.* This graceful swan from the Old World is now established locally as a feral species in several parts of North America, notably within the area from the New England States to Chesapeake Bay on the east, to Minnesota and Missouri on the west. Some of the birds, no doubt, were introduced while others were escapees from zoos. (Shown here is an immature.) 152 cm. (60″)

Chapter 8

SOME INTERESTING SIDELIGHTS

The number of bird species extant in the world today is believed to be between eight and nine thousand. The images of several hundred species have been memorialized on postage stamps in more than one hundred and fifty countries. Every state in the United States has selected a "state" bird, several states picking such species as the Northern Cardinal, Northern Mockingbird, and Western Meadowlark. The United States chose the Bald Eagle in 1782 as its national emblem. Many religious organizations use the dove as a symbol of the Holy Spirit. Illustrations of birds appear on such items of trade as jewelry, dishes, and stationery. Recently, many species served as "guinea pigs" in connection with the danger of DDT to human beings.

Our use of birds as food cannot be overlooked. In the domestic category, farmyard chickens are believed to be derived from the Red Junglefowl of India and neighboring countries. The farmyard goose may be derived from the Greylag Goose of the Old World. Use of the farmyard Mallard dates back for many centuries. In the Western Hemisphere it is believed that certain farmyard ducks were derived from the Muscovy Duck. Domestic turkeys are the descendants of the Wild Turkey.

The Common Eider has furnished large quantities of "eider down" for commercial use. It is not gathered from the bird, but from the nest. Permits are required. Birds such as parrots, mynas, crows, and magpies have been trained to talk for indoor entertainment.

Efforts have been made to release many foreign species into the wilds of North America. We now find the following: House Sparrow, European Starling, Rock Dove, Ring-necked Pheasant, Gray Partridge, Chukar, Black Francolin, Spotted Dove, Ringed Turtle-Dove, Eurasian Skylark, Spot-breasted Oriole, Java Sparrow, Eurasian Tree Sparrow, and Mute Swan. A good example of a species which apparently came of its own accord is the Cattle Egret. Many efforts to release birds have met with failure, and it may be just as well that they have, for not all species are desirable. One example of an unwanted species is the Monk Parakeet of South America, as it is a consumer of fruit and grain.

As of this writing, the House Finch, which was released on Long Island in 1940, has spread widely in the eastern states and provinces, and will, no doubt, join its western counterparts in the near future. Some observers believe that it gives the House Sparrow a lot of competition during the nesting season.

Efforts to restore the numbers of California Condor took on a new twist during the early 1980's, when personnel of the San Diego Zoo began hatching and rearing young condors. They are able to do this work, but the cost of food is a problem. They feed the nestlings skinned mice, among other things.

For many years the Whooping Crane has been limited to the flyway from the Wood Buffalo National Park and vicinity in Canada, to the Aransas National Wildlife Refuge and vicinity of Texas. In order to give the species a better chance of survival, wildlife workers are now trying to establish at least one additional flyway. The points would be from Gray's Lake National Wildlife Refuge in southeastern Idaho to such points as central New Mexico, northwestern Mexico, or central California. Sandhill Cranes hatch the eggs of the Whooping Crane and rear the chicks as though they were their own. To use a few eggs in this experiment is not a drain on the population of the original flyway as Whooping Cranes seem to be able to rear only one of the two chicks which they normally hatch. In addition to the wild eggs used, a few have been produced on the Patuxent Wildlife Research Center, Laurel, Maryland, by a small captive flock of Whooping Cranes.

Appendix A

MAN-MADE NESTING DEVICES

Listed below are details for a variety of man-made nesting devices such as bird houses, shelves, bark slabs, cleats, wire saucers, open-top boxes, hollow trees, and platforms.

Most of the birds known to use such devices are listed in alphabetical order, but I have omitted a few species which have rarely been found to avail themselves of man's help. These include Burrowing Owl, Western Kingbird, Northern Mockingbird, Brown Thrasher, American Dipper, Orchard Oriole, Northern Oriole (including Baltimore and Bullock's), and Common Grackle. No doubt, others could be added to this list.

In addition to the specifications which follow, I have added some notes on the preferred habitat of the species involved; also a few remarks on their habits.

Most houses can be mounted on posts or the trunks of trees; some can be mounted on the walls of buildings. Except where otherwise specified, they can be situated in either sun or shade. Those devices that have no roofs will gather water, so a few holes should be bored in the floor.

MAN-MADE NESTING DEVICES

(Note: 2.54 centimeters = 1 inch; .3048 meter = 1 foot; .9144 meter = 1 yard)

	Device Type	Floor Inside	Entrance Diameter	Entrance Above Floor	Place Above Ground	Habitat & Remarks
Barn-Owl, Common	Open-top box	46 x 46 cm.		sides 46 cm. tall	3—6 m.	Attach inside old building in darkest parts, but accessible to open window. 20 cm. clearance above box. Sawdust needed.
Bluebird, Eastern	House	11 x 11 cm.	3.8 cm.	20 cm.	1.5—3 m.	Favors open lawn type for feeding, scattered trees.
Bluebird, Mountain	House	13 x 13 cm.	4.1 cm.	20 cm.	1.5—3 m.	Partly wooded habitat, favors the higher altitudes.
Bluebird, Western	House	11 x 11 cm.	3.8 cm.	20 cm.	1.5—3 m.	Habitat open, scattered trees; breeding range includes the lower altitudes.
Bufflehead	House	23 x 23 cm.	8.3 cm.	38 cm.	3—6 m.	Likes open forest, near water, houses serve best over water. Add sawdust.
Chickadee, Black-capped	House	10 x 10 cm.	2.9 cm.	13 cm.	1.5—3 m.	Wooded, or partly wooded area. Birch-bark houses favored in some regions.
Chickadee, Boreal	House	10 x 10 cm.	2.5 cm.	13 cm.	1.5—3 m.	Wooded or shrubby habitat. Often found in bogs.
Chickadee, Carolina	House	10 x 10 cm.	2.5 cm.	13 cm.	1.5—3 m.	Wooded, or partly wooded habitat. Appears to be nonmigratory.
Chickadee, Chestnut-backed	House	10 x 10 cm.	2.5 cm.	13 cm.	1.5—3 m.	Wooded habitat, especially coniferous. A bird of the humid coastal forests.
Chickadee, Mexican	House	10 x 10 cm.	2.5 cm.	13 cm.	1.5—3 m.	Partly wooded habitat. Often in the higher elevations.
Chickadee, Mountain	House	10 x 10 cm.	2.5 cm.	13 cm.	1.5—3 m.	Wooded habitat, including coniferous. Occurs above timber line.
Cormorant, Double-crested	Platform	76 x 76 cm.			3—6 m.	Heron colony and similar habitat. Mount on tree or post in sun. Birds are colonial.
Cormorant, Great	Platform	76 x 76 cm.			3—6 m.	Seacoast habitat. Mount on post in sun. Birds are colonial.

Species	Nest type	Floor	Depth	Entrance above floor	Height	Notes
Cormorant, Olivaceous	Platform	76 x 76 cm.			3–6 m.	Likes Mangrove trees. Mount on tree or post, in sun; in either salt- or fresh-water habitat.
Creeper, Brown	Bark slab	6 x 8 cm.		likes roof	2–6 m.	Found in forest. Attach to trunk of tree.
Dove, Mourning (plus other tree-nesting doves)	Wire saucer	25 cm. diameter			2–6 m.	Scattered tree, varied habitat. Attach saucer to strong fork in tree (in shade). Remove branches on two sides annually for flying clearance. Throw out old nests yearly.
Duck, Wood	House	25 x 25 cm.	7.6 cm. tall x 10.2 cm. w.	46 cm.	3–8 m.	Partly wooded habitat, also open marsh. Houses serve best over water; two or three per acre. Add sawdust.
Egret, Great (possibly herons also)	Platform	76 x 76 cm.			any height	Open water habitat; also among trees. Individual platforms above water's surface or in trees. If for colony can be a swim pier.
Finch, House	House	15 x 15 cm.	5.1 cm.	10 cm.	1.5–3 m.	Residential habitat, partly wooded. Range is expanding.
Flicker, Northern (include Yellow-shafted, Red-shafted and Gilded)	House	20 x 20 cm.	7.6 cm.	38 cm.	2–6 m.	Partly wooded habitat, can survive where trees are sparse. Gilded in desert.
Flycatcher, Ash-throated	House	15 x 15 cm.	5.1 cm.	20 cm.	2–6 m.	Wooded, or partly wooded habitat. Breeding range includes the deserts.
Flycatcher, Brown-crested (formerly Wied's)	House	15 x 15 cm.	5.1 cm.	20 cm.	2–6 m.	Desert habitat, or wooded. Not reclusive.
Flycatcher, Dusky-capped (formerly Olivaceous)	House	13 x 13 cm.	5.1 cm.	20 cm.	2–6 m.	Wooded, or shrubby habitat. Away from disturbances, in shade.
Flycatcher, Great Crested	House	15 x 15 cm.	5.1 cm.	20 cm.	2–6 m.	Wooded habitat, or partly wooded, away from disturbances.
Flycatcher, Sulphur-bellied	House	15 x 15 cm.	5.1 cm.	20 cm.	3–6 m.	Partly wooded habitat. Builds nest to level of entrance.
Flycatcher, Western	Open shelf	13 x 13 cm.		roof 13 cm, above floor	2–3 m.	Deciduous forest habitat, near water. Attach on tree in shade. Bird has strong homing instinct.
Goldeneye, Barrow's	House	25 x 25 cm.	9 cm. tall x 11.4 cm. w.	46 cm.	3–6 m.	Open forest area, with water. Houses best over water.

	Device Type	Floor Inside	Entrance Diameter	Entrance Above Floor	Place Above Ground	Habitat & Remarks
Goldeneye, Common	House	25 x 25 cm.	9 cm. tall x 11.4 cm. w.	46 cm.	3–6 m.	Forest habitat, near water. Open-top houses are preferred, although standard type is used. Make of wood.
Goose, Canada (not for ducks)	Floating platform (but anchored)	76 x 76 cm.			5–15 m.	Open water or tree stub habitat. One-half barrel is best on water; tub is satisfactory atop tree stub. Place devices in sun not farther from shore than 91.5 m., nor closer together than 61 m.
Hawk-Owl, Northern	House	23 x 23 cm.	8.9 cm.	51 cm.	3–6 m.	Coniferous forest habitat; muskeg. A diurnal species.
Kestrel, American	House	20 x 20 cm.	7.6 cm.	25 cm.	2–6 m.	Open, or partly wooded habitat. Add sawdust. May be found in city suburbs.
Martin, Purple	House	15 x 15 cm.	6.4 cm.	6 cm.	4–6 m.	Open habitat, scattered trees. Compartments, 15 cm. high; attic helps cool.
Merganser, Common	House	33 x 33 cm.	12.7 cm.	63.5 cm.	3–6 m.	Chiefly a fresh-water species, in or near forest.
Merganser, Hooded	House	25 x 25 cm.	7.6 cm. tall x 10.2 cm.w.	46 cm.	3–8 m.	Wooded stream or lake habitat; chiefly a fresh-water species.
Myna, Crested	House	18 x 18 cm.	6.4 cm.	20 cm.	3–6 m.	City habitat; partly wooded. Restricted range.
Nuthatch, Brown-headed	House	10 x 10 cm.	3.2 cm.	15 cm.	1.5–6 m.	Partly wooded habitat, especially pine. Appears to be nonmigratory.
Nuthatch, Pigmy	House	10 x 10 cm.	3.2 cm.	20 cm.	3–6 m.	Wooded habitat, especially conifers. Breeding range includes the mountains.
Nuthatch, Red-breasted	House	10 x 10 cm.	3.2 cm.	15 cm.	1.5–6 m.	Wooded habitat, especially coniferous. Bird may smear resin around house entrance.
Nuthatch, White-breasted	House	11 x 11 cm.	3.8 cm.	15 cm.	1.5–6 m.	Partly wooded habitat. Favors deciduous trees of the climax stage.
Osprey	Carriage-wheel	76 x 76 cm.			3–6 m.	Open or wooded habitat. Mount atop post, over, or near water in sun. Add nest sticks to attract bird's attention. Nest must be higher than nearby trees. Birds are loosely colonial.
Owl, Barred	Hollow tree	33 x 38 cm.		51 cm.	6–15 m.	Wooded, often lowland habitat. Construct as hollow tree and mount on tree in shade. Add sawdust. Entry is from above.

	Device Type	Floor Inside	Entrance Diameter	Entrance Above Floor	Place Above Ground	Habitat & Remarks
Owl, Boreal	House	18 x 18 cm.	7.6 cm.	38 cm.	3–6 m.	Coniferous forest habitat. Favors mature spruce forests.
Owl, Elf	House	13 x 13 cm.	5.1 cm.	22 cm.	3–6 m.	Cactus; scattered tree habitat. Breeding range is mostly desert.
Owl, Flammulated	House	13 x 13 cm.	5.1 cm.	20 cm.	3–6 m.	Wooded habitat, especially pine. Breeding range includes the mountains.
Owl, Northern Saw-whet	House	15 x 15 cm.	6.4 cm.	25 cm.	2–6 m.	Partly wooded habitat; coniferous swamp. Breeding range includes the mountains.
Owl, Spotted	House	25 x 25 cm.	10.2 cm.	63.5 cm.	5–6 m.	Coniferous forest habitat, favors mature Douglas fir.
Phoebe, Eastern	Open shelf	15 x 15 cm.		roof 15 cm. above floor	2–3 m.	Partly wooded habitat; mud needed. Attach on wall, 15 cm. below eaves, in shade.
Phoebe, Say's	Open shelf	15 x 15 cm.		roof 15 cm. above floor	2–3 m.	Varied habitat; mud not needed. Attach on wall 15 cm. below eaves.
Pygmy-Owl, Ferruginous	House	13 x 13 cm.	5.1 cm.	20 cm.	3–6 m.	Desert habitat, wooded canyon. Diurnal in habits.
Pygmy-Owl, Northern	House	13 x 13 cm.	5.1 cm.	20 cm.	3–6 m.	Partly wooded habitat. Breeding range includes the mountains.
Robin, American	Open shelf	18 x 18 cm.		roof 20 cm. above floor	2–6 m.	Habitat varied; mud needed. Attach on wall, 20 cm. below eaves.
Sapsucker, Red-breasted	House	13 x 13 cm.	4.4 cm.	25 cm.	2–6 m.	Wooded, or partly wooded habitat. Often found in aspen stands.
Sapsucker, Williamson's	House	13 x 13 cm.	4.4 cm.	25 cm.	2–6 m.	Open coniferous habitat. Breeding range includes the mountains.
Sapsucker, Yellow-bellied	House	13 x 13 cm.	4.4 cm.	25 cm.	2–6 m.	Wooded, or partly wooded habitat. Favors damp spots.
Screech-Owl, Eastern	House	18 x 18 cm.	7.6 cm.	25 cm.	3–6 m.	Partly wooded habitat. May be found in city suburbs.
Screech-Owl, Western	House	20 x 20 cm.	8.9 cm.	30.5 cm.	3–6 m.	Partly wooded habitat. Considerable variation in size and color of birds.

	Device Type	Floor Inside	Entrance Diameter	Entrance Above Floor	Place Above Ground	Habitat & Remarks
Screech-Owl, Whiskered	House	13 x 13 cm.	5.1 cm.	25 cm.	2—6 m.	Partly wooded habitat. Breeding range includes high altitudes.
Sparrow, Eurasian Tree	House	13 x 13 cm.	3.8 cm.	20 cm.	1.5—3 m.	Residential; partly wooded. Restricted range; not aggressive.
Sparrow, House	House	13 x 13 cm.	3.8 cm.	20 cm.	1.5—3 m.	Found about buildings, partly wooded. Species usually undesirable; research may be useful.
Sparrow, Song	Open shelf	15 x 15 cm.		roof 15 cm. above floor	1—1.5 m.	Brushy habitat, often wet. Attach on wall in shade. Bird has strong homing instinct.
Starling, European	House	15 x 15 cm.	5.1 cm.	20 cm.	3—6 m.	Partly wooded habitat. Species undesirable; research may be useful.
Swallow, Barn	Open shelf; or cleat	15 x 15 cm.		roof 15 cm. above floor	2—6 m.	Likes farm buildings, bridges. Attach on wall, 25 cm. below eaves. Mud needed.
Swallow, Cliff	Cleat				6 m.	Habitat: farm building; bridge. Mud needed for globular shaped nests. If building is painted attach long unpainted strips horizontally to wall, within 1 m. of overhanging roof.
Swallow, Tree	House	13 x 13 cm.	3.8 cm.	20 cm.	1.5—3 m.	Open habitat; near, or over water. Colonial.
Swallow, Violet-green	House	13 x 13 cm.	3.8 cm.	20 cm.	1.5—3 m.	Open habitat, near or over water. Colonial.
Swift, Chimney	Hollow tree	38 cm. inside diameter				Varied habitat; including urban. Tree is hollow to ground. Birds attach nests to vertical surface inside. Birds enter from above. Build tall tree.
Swift, Vaux's	Hollow tree	38 cm. inside diameter				Wooded habitat. See Chimney Swift.
Tit, Siberian (formerly Gray-headed Chickadee)	House	10 x 10 cm.	3.2 cm.	13 cm.	1.5—3 m.	Partly wooded habitat. Breeding range includes high altitudes.
Titmouse, Bridled	House	10 x 10 cm.	3.2 cm.	15 cm.	1.5—3 m.	Partly wooded habitat. Breeding range includes the mountains.
Titmouse, Plain	House	10 x 10 cm.	3.2 cm.	15 cm.	1.5—3 m.	Wooded, or partly wooded habitat.
Titmouse, Tufted	House	10 x 10 cm.	3.2 cm.	15 cm.	1.5—3 m.	Partly wooded habitat. A.O.U. combines Black-crested Titmouse here.

	Device Type	Floor Inside	Entrance Diameter	Entrance Above Floor	Place Above Ground	Habitat & Remarks
Trogon, Elegant (formerly called "Coppery-tailed")	Hollow tree	20 x 20 cm. inside				3–6 m.	Wooded habitat. Hollow about 25 cm. deep. Entry from above. Mount on tree.
Warbler, Lucy's	House	10 x 10 cm.	2.9 cm.	13 cm.	1.5–3 m.	Partly wooded habitat, especially mesquite. Not closely dependent upon enclosures.
Warbler, Prothonotary	House	10 x 10 cm.	2.9 cm.	20 cm.	1.5–3 m.	Wooded habitat, often swamps. Locate house in shade. A restless species on breeding grounds.
Whistling-Duck, Black-bellied	House	25 x 25 cm.	12.7 cm.	46 cm.	3–6 m.	Open forest habitat, with water. Houses may be away from water, or over water. Add sawdust.
Woodpecker, Acorn	House	13 x 13 cm.	5.1 cm.	25 cm.	2–6 m.	Partly wooded, especially oak habitat. Birds are communal in nesting habits.
Woodpecker, Black-backed	House	13 x 13 cm.	4.4 cm.	25 cm.	2–6 m.	Coniferous forest, including tamarack habitat. May be local in distribution.
Woodpecker, Downy	House	10 x 10 cm.	3.2 cm.	20 cm.	1.5–6 m.	Wooded, or partly wooded habitat. Prefers deciduous type.
Woodpecker, Gila	House	15 x 15 cm.	5.1 cm.	30.5 cm.	2–6 m.	Cactus, scattered tree area. Breeding range is mostly desert.
Woodpecker, Golden-fronted	House	15 x 15 cm.	5.1 cm.	30.5 cm.	2–6 m.	Wooded or partly wooded habitat. Favors deciduous type.
Woodpecker, Hairy	House	13 x 13 cm.	5.1 cm.	25 cm.	1.5–6 m.	Wooded, or partly wooded habitat, away from disturbances.
Woodpecker, Ladder-backed	House	13 x 13 cm.	4.4 cm.	25 cm.	2–6 m.	Partly wooded, desert, varied habitat.
Woodpecker, Lewis'	House	15 x 15 cm.	6.4 cm.	25 cm.	2–6 m.	Partly wooded habitat. Either deciduous or coniferous type.
Woodpecker, Nuttall's	House	13 x 13 cm.	3.8 cm.	25 cm.	2–6 m.	Partly wooded, especially oak habitat. Favors deciduous trees.
Woodpecker, Pileated	House	23 x 23 cm.	8.9 cm.	63.5 cm.	4–6 m.	Extensive woodland habitat, away from disturbances.

	Device Type	Floor Inside	Entrance Diameter	Entrance Above Floor	Place Above Ground	Habitat & Remarks
Woodpecker, Red-bellied	House	15 x 15 cm.	5.1 cm.	25 cm.	2—6 m.	Wooded, or partly wooded habitat; favors deciduous type in North.
Woodpecker, Red-cockaded	House	13 x 13 cm.	4.4 cm.	25 cm.	3—6 m.	Open pine habitat. To smear face of house with resin may help.
Woodpecker, Red-headed	House	13 x 13 cm.	5.1 cm.	25 cm.	2—6 m.	Partly wooded habitat, favors oaks.
Woodpecker, Strickland's (formerly Arizona Woodpecker)	House	13 x 13 cm.	4.4 cm.	25 cm.	2—6 m.	Partly wooded habitat. Breeding range includes the mountains.
Woodpecker, Three-toed	House	13 x 13 cm.	3.8 cm.	25 cm.	2—6 m.	Coniferous forest habitat. Often in burned over areas.
Woodpecker, White-headed	House	13 x 13 cm.	5.1 cm.	25 cm.	2—6 m.	Pine and sequoia. Breeding range includes the mountains.
Wren, Bewick's	House	10 x 10 cm.	2.9 cm.	13 cm.	1.5—3 m.	Partly wooded; village type habitat. Away from disturbances.
Wren, Canyon	Open shelf	15 x 15 cm.		roof 15 cm. above floor	2—3 m.	Habitat varied, residential. Attach on wall or post. Breeding range includes mountains.
Wren, Carolina	Open-top box	10 x 10 cm.		10 cm. sides	1.5—3 m.	Partly wooded habitat; thicket. Attach on porch wall, or on inside wall of old building 10 cm. clearance above box.
Wren, House	House	10 x 10 cm.	2.5 cm.	13 cm.	1.5—2 m.	Not particular, but likes cover. Will fill all houses; not wanted near bluebird.
Wren, Rock	Open shelf	15 x 20 cm.		roof 15 cm. above floor	2—3 m.	Varied habitat, barren land. Attach on wall. Longest dimension holds the pebbles the birds usually bring in.

Appendix B

PLANTS THAT FURNISH FOOD

Listed below are some of the plants or groups of plants that are popular with birds. Seasons when the food is available are indicated, and the names of a few birds are supplied to furnish an idea of what to expect. Bear in mind that certain plant foods relished by birds in one part of the country may be totally neglected in another part. The birds may not be adapted to them, or they may have a substitute food which they like better.

In order that plants can be found with ease, I have included the genus and family for each of the categories listed. My nomenclature follows that used by Britton and Brown in their three volume work, *An Illustrated Flora of the Northern United States and Canada* (second edition), except for one plant, the Pepper-tree. Nomenclature for it is that used by Norman Taylor, editor of *The Practical Encyclopedia of Gardening.*

Instead of listing the plants according to their structure, I have started each group with some of the most popular varieties, and omitted those plants which normally are cultivated to produce food for human consumption. Poison sumac and poison ivy are left out although the latter is a valuable source of food in winter for many species of birds.

It is understood that everyone will consult the local laws regarding importations, disease problems, and the like. Examples of plants that may be objectionable to man's interests are the following: barberry (wheat rust); buckthorn (oak rust); currant (white pine rust); junipers are not wanted near orchards; and pepper-trees should not be planted near orange groves. Some plants not wanted within the reach of cattle are: rhododendron, laurel, yew, groundsel, lupine, nightshade, and certain wild cherries.

Trees and Shrubs

Crab Apples: *Malus;* Malaceae. Utilized in spring, autumn, and winter by approximately fifty species of birds, among which are thrushes, waxwings, grosbeaks, woodpeckers, towhees, meadowlarks, titmice, and grouse.

Mountain Ashes: *Sorbus;* Malaceae. Utilized in summer, autumn, and winter by more than fifteen species of birds, among which are grosbeaks, thrushes, tanagers, waxwings, catbirds, woodpeckers, orioles, and thrashers.

Choke-berries: *Aronia;* Malaceae. Utilized in summer, autumn, and winter by more than twenty-five species of birds, among which are chickadees, thrashers, meadowlarks, thrushes, waxwings, tanagers flycatchers, and vireos.

June-berries (Serviceberry, Shad-bush): *Amelanchier;* Malaceae. Utilized in summer, autumn, and winter by more than forty-five species of birds, among which are thrushes, orioles, waxwings, grosbeaks, woodpeckers, catbirds, flycatchers, and thrashers.

Thorn-apples (Hawthorns): *Crataegus;* Malaceae. Utilized in spring, autumn, and winter by more than forty species of birds, among which are grosbeaks, thrushes, sparrows, woodpeckers, waxwings, flycatchers, finches, and grouse.

Mulberries: *Morus;* Moraceae. Utilized in summer by approximately sixty species of birds, among which are warblers, vireos, tanagers, orioles, cuckoos, titmice, thrushes, waxwings, grosbeaks, woodpeckers, catbirds, and flycatchers.

Wild Cherries (Choke Cherry, Black Cherry): *Padus;* Amygdalaceae. Utilized in summer and autumn by approximately seventy-five species of birds, among which are thrushes, waxwings, woodpeckers, tanagers, flycatchers, finches, grouse, orioles, doves, quail, catbirds, and grosbeaks.

Sumacs: *Rhus;* Anacardiaceae. Utilized throughout the year by approximately one-hundred species of birds, among which are wrentits, mockingbirds, flycatchers, woodpeckers, thrushes, chickadees, quail, grouse, and grosbeaks.

Plums and Sand Cherries: *Prunus;* Amygdalaceae. Utilized in summer and autumn by more than fifteen species of birds, among which are towhees, finches, woodpeckers, and grosbeaks.

Elderberries: *Sambucus;* Caprifoliaceae. Utilized in summer and autumn by approximately one-hundred and twenty species of birds, among which are wrens, phainopeplas, finches, woodpeckers, sparrows, towhees, flycatchers, thrushes, grosbeaks, and wrentits.

Viburnums (High Bush-cranberry, Nanny-berry): *Viburnum;* Caprifoliaceae. Utilized throughout the year by more than forty species of birds, among which are vireos, cuckoos, catbirds, waxwings, thrashers, finches, thrushes, and grosbeaks.

Snowberries (Coral-berry, Wolfberry): *Symphoricarpos;* Caprifoliaceae. Utilized throughout the year by more than forty species of birds, among which are grosbeaks, wrentits, towhees, flycatchers, thrushes, and vireos.

Honeysuckles: *Lonicera;* Caprifoliaceae. Utilized in summer, autumn and winter by more than twenty-five species of birds, among which are hummingbirds, thrushes, grosbeaks, vireos, catbirds, waxwings, towhees, and quail.

Dogwoods (Cornel): *Cornus;* Cornaceae. Utilized in summer, autumn, and winter by approximately one-hundred species of birds, among which are mockingbirds, flycatchers, woodpeckers, swallows, thrushes, grosbeaks, sparrows, vireos, finches, titmice, quail, and grouse.

Tupelos (Sour Gum): *Nyssa;* Cornaceae. Utilized throughout the year by more than forty species of birds, among which are woodpeckers, mockingbirds, waxwings, thrushes, finches, thrashers, and catbirds.

Oaks: *Quercus;* Fagaceae. Utilized in fall and winter by approximately sixty-five species of birds, among which are jays, woodpeckers, nuthatches, thrashers, grosbeaks, thrushes, meadowlarks, wrens, and towhees.

Hollies (Winterberry, Inkberry): *Ilex;* Ilicaceae. Utilized throughout the year by approximately fifty species of birds, among which are thrushes, woodpeckers, mockingbirds, towhees, thrashers, waxwings, grosbeaks, grouse, and quail.

Bayberries (Waxberry): *Myrica;* Myricacea. Utilized throughout the year by approximately ninety species of birds, among which are swallows, warblers, thrushes, vireos, flycatchers, wrens, flickers, quail, wrentits, mockingbirds, catbirds, and waterfowl.

Blueberries (Whortleberry, Bilberry): *Vaccinium;* Vacciniaceae. Utilized in summer by approximately ninety-five species of birds, among which are titmice, thrushes, towhees, thrashers, sparrows, flycatchers, grosbeaks, orioles, quail, and grouse.

Huckleberries: *Gaylussacia;* Vacciniaceae. Utilized in summer and autumn by approximately fifty species of birds, among which are towhees, tanagers, grosbeaks, woodpeckers, thrushes, catbirds, flycatchers, and mockingbirds.

Buffalo-berries: *Lepargyraea;* Elaeagnaceae. Utilized in summer, autumn, and winter by more than twenty species of birds, among which are grosbeaks, thrushes, catbirds, woodpeckers, thrashers, and grouse.

Roses: *Rosa;* Rosaceae. Utilized throughout the year by more than forty-five species of birds, among which are finches, thrushes, vireos, grosbeaks, buntings, chickadees, waxwings, mockingbirds, quail, and grouse.

Spruces: *Picea;* Pinaceae. Utilized in fall and winter by more than thirty-five species of birds, among which are crossbills, grosbeaks, woodpeckers, chickadees, thrushes, and flycatchers.

Junipers: *Juniperus;* Pinaceae. Utilized throughout the year by approximately fifty-five species of birds, among which are thrushes, warblers, waxwings, grosbeaks, flycatchers, swallows, finches, mockingbirds, and woodpeckers.

Pines: *Pinus;* Pinaceae. Utilized in spring, autumn, and winter by approximately sixty-five species of birds, among which are crossbills, grosbeaks, finches, woodpeckers, nuthatches, chickadees, and meadowlarks.

Firs (Balsam): *Abies;* Pinaceae. Utilized in spring and winter by more than fifteen species of birds, among which are crossbills, chickadees, and finches.

Hemlocks: *Tauga;* Pinaceae. Utilized in winter by more than ten species of birds among which are crossbills, finches, woodpeckers, and chickadees.

Poplars (Aspen, Cottonwood): *Populus;* Salicaceae. Utilized in spring and winter by more than fifteen species of birds, among which are grosbeaks, grouse, and finches.

Willows: *Salix;* Salicaceae. Utilized throughout the year by by more than twenty species of birds, among which are grosbeaks and finches.

Hackberries (Sugar-berry): *Celtis;* Ulmaceae. Utilized throughout the year by approximately fifty species of birds, among which are thrushes, mockingbirds, woodpeckers, towhees, flycatchers, and finches.

Bermuda Mulberries: *Callicarpa;* Verbenaceae. Utilized in autumn and winter by more than fifteen species of birds, among which are thrushes, towhees, thrashers, grosbeaks, vireos, catbirds, and mockingbirds.

Birches: *Betula;* Betulaceae. Utilized in autumn and winter by more than thirty species of birds, among which are finches, chickadees, sparrows, and juncos.

Alders: *Alnus;* Betulaceae. Utilized in autumn and winter by more than twenty-five species of birds, among which are finches and sparrows.

Spice-bushes (Spice-wood): *Benzoin;* Lauraceae. Utilized in summer and autumn by more than twenty species of birds, among which are flycatchers, thrushes, vireos, catbirds, woodpeckers, and grosbeaks.

Sassafras (Ague Tree): Sassafras; Lauraceae. Utilized in summer and autumn by more than twenty species of birds, among which are woodpeckers, vireos, flycatchers, thrushes, catbirds, and quail.

Silver-berries: *Elaeagnus;* Elaeagnaceae. Utilized in autumn and winter by more than fifteen species of birds, among which are grosbeaks, thrushes, juncos, towhees, sparrows, finches, waxwings, and grouse.

Persimmons: *Diospyros;* Ebenaceae. Utilized in spring, autumn, and winter by more than ten species of birds, among which are thrushes, flycatchers, woodpeckers, and mockingbirds.

Euonymi (Wahoo, Spindle-tree): *Euonymus;* Celastraceae. Utilized in winter by more than ten species of birds, among which are thrushes, tanagers, and woodpeckers.

Larches (Tamarack): *Larix;* Pinaceae. Utilized in autumn and winter by more than five species of birds, among which are crossbills and finches.

Arbor Vitae (White Cedar): *Thuja;* Pinaceae. Utilized in autumn and winter by more than five species of birds, among which are grosbeaks, thrushes, and towhees.

Yews (Ground-hemlock): *Taxus;* Taxaceae. Utilized in autumn and winter by more than five species of birds, among which are thrushes.

Beeches: *Fagus;* Fagaceae. Utilized in autumn and winter by more than ten species of birds, among which are jays, woodpeckers, and nuthatches.

Maples and Box Elders: *Acer;* Aceraceae. Utilized in spring, autumn, and winter by more than five species of birds, among which are grosbeaks and finches.

Buckthorns (Dwarf Alder): *Rhamnus;* Rhamnaceae. Utilized in spring, autumn, and winter by more than twenty species of birds, among which are phainopeplas, flycatchers, wrentits, catbirds, woodpeckers, thrashers, and thrushes.

Barberries: *Berberis;* Berberidaceae. Utilized throughout the year by more than fifteen species of birds, among which are waxwings, thrushes, woodpeckers, and catbirds.

Pepper-trees (Mastic-tree): *Schinus;* Anacardiaceae. Utilized in autumn and winter by more than fifteen species of birds, among which are waxwings, thrushes, phainopeplas, finches, and mockingbirds.

Privets: *Ligustrum;* Oleaceae. Utilized in summer, autumn, and winter by more than fifteen species of birds, among which are robins, mockingbirds, warblers, and finches.

Vines

Trumpet-creepers (Trumpet-vine): *Bignonia;* Bignoniaceae. Utilized by hummingbirds in spring.

Wild Grapes (Fox-Grape, Frost Grape): *Vitis;* Vitaceae. Utilized in summer and autumn by approximately ninety species of birds, among which are thrushes, grosbeaks, woodpeckers, catbirds, flycatchers, sparrows, grouse, and quail.

Virginia Creepers (Ivy): *Parthenocissus;* Vitaceae. Utilized in summer, autumn, and winter by more than forty species of birds, among which are mockingbirds, thrushes, woodpeckers, thrashers, vireos, catbirds, titmice, and tanagers.

Greenbriars (Catbriar): *Smilax;* Smilaceae. Utilized throughout the year by more than forty-five species of birds, among which are mockingbirds, thrushes, grosbeaks, catbirds, thrashers, and quail.

Supple-jacks (Rattan-vine): *Berchemia;* Rhamnaceae. Utilized in summer by more than fifteen species of birds, among which are horned larks, mockingbirds, thrushes, and thrashers.

Moonseeds: *Epibaterium;* Menispermaceae. Utilized in summer and autumn by more than five species of birds, among which are mockingbirds, thrashers, and catbirds.

Bittersweets: *Celastrus;* Celastraceae. Utilized in spring, autumn, and winter by more than ten species of birds, among which are vireos and thrushes.

Herbaceous Shrubs

Poke-berries (Inkberry): *Phytolacca;* Phytolaccaceae. Utilized in summer, autumn, and winter by approximately fifty-five species of birds, among which are doves, thrushes, flycatchers, mockingbirds, catbirds, woodpeckers, and grosbeaks.

Spikenards (Sarsaparilla): *Aralia;* Araliaceae. Utilized in summer and autumn by more than twenty species of birds, among which are nuthatches, thrushes, grosbeaks, quail, meadowlarks, woodpeckers, sparrows, and catbirds.

Crowberries (Heathberry): *Empetrum* Empetraceae. Utilized throughout the year by more than forty-five species of birds, among which are buntings, grosbeaks, and sparrows.

Ground Cover

Partridge-berries (Twin-berry): *Mitchella;* Rubiaceae. Utilized throughout the year by more than fifteen species of birds, among which are thrushes, catbirds, thrashers, and grouse.

Bearberries (Kinnikinic): *Uva-ursi;* Ericaceae. Utilized throughout the year by more than fifteen species of birds, among which are wrentits, quail, grosbeaks, sparrows, thrashers, grouse, and mockingbirds.

Wintergreens (Checker-berry): *Gaultheria;* Ericaceae. Utilized throughout the year by more than fifteen species of birds, among which are thrashers, wrentits, thrushes, and grosbeaks.

Selected Bibliography

American Ornithologists' Union Committee. 1983. *Check-List of North American Birds.* Sixth Edition. The American Ornithologists' Union.

Bent, A.C. et al. 1919-1968. *Life Histories of North American Birds.* 23 vols. U.S. National Museum, Washington.

Leopold, A. 1933. *Game Management.* Charles Scribner's Sons, New York.

Linduska, J.P., Ed. 1964. *Waterfowl Tomorrow.* U.S. Department of the Interior Fish and Wildlife Service, Washington.

Madson, John. 1978. *The Mourning Dove.* Winchester Press, New York.

Mathews, F.S. 1909. *Field Book of Wild Birds and Their Music.* G.P. Putnam's Sons, New York.

Palmer, R.S., Ed. 1962. *Handbook of North American Birds.* Vol. 1. Yale University Press, New Haven.

Reed, C.A. 1965. *North American Bird's Eggs.* Revised by P.A. Buckley. Dover Publications, Inc., New York.

Sanderson, G.C., Ed. 1977. *Management of Migratory Shore and Upland Game Birds in North America.* The International Association of Fish and Wildlife Agencies, Washington.

Smith, D.R., Coordinator. 1975. *Symposium on Management of Forest and Range Habitats for Nongame Birds.* Forest Service, U.S. Department of Agriculture, Washington.

Sutton, G.M. 1967. *Oklahoma Birds.* University of Oklahoma Press, Norman.

Terres, J.K. 1968. *Songbirds in Your Garden.* Thomas Y. Crowell Co., New York.

Welty, J.C. 1962. *The Life of Birds.* W. B. Saunders Co., Philadelphia.

Selected Periodicals of Ornithological Societies

American Birds, National Audubon Society, 950 Third Ave., New York, N.Y. 10022

The Auk, The American Ornithologists' Union.

The Condor, Cooper Ornithological Society.

Wilson Bulletin, Wilson Ornithological Society.